Simple Pleasures

From Our Table To Yours

ARAB MOTHERS' CLUB • ARAB, AL

Arab Mothers' Club

Additional copies may be obtained at the cost of $16.95 each,
plus $3.50 shipping and handling, each book.

Send to:

Simple Pleasures

Arab Mothers' Club
P.O. Box 884
Arab, Alabama 35016

ISBN: 0-9662196-0-0

First Printing   2,000   November, 1998

Printed in the USA by

WIMMER
The Wimmer Companies
Memphis
1-800-548-2537

Simple Pleasures...

Family. Fellowship. Food. Fun.

These simple words evoke the essence of the things we treasure. The simple pleasures. This cookbook contains recipes for celebrating with families, for entertaining friends. It features many different types of recipes and food: simple to scrumptious to sophisticated. Add festivity and fun for a perfect occasion!

Family. Family includes not only those that live in our own homes but also our extended family — all the uncles and aunts and cousins (no matter how many times removed!). Our large collection of kissing cousins means that most friends are at least distantly related to us — so our extended family is quite large.

Fellowship. Arab is fellowship: visiting, sharing, caring. In a community as closely-knit as ours, fellowship is an important part of all our daily activities. Stopping at the grocery store, fixing supper for a sick friend, sharing potluck dinners at church, lounging on lazy summer afternoons at the lake, gathering to watch 'the game' — we are sure to find fellowship in even the most simple of our routine activities.

Food. And lots of it! In all different settings and for all different occasions, food is part of the celebration of life. From breakfast brunches, to children's birthday parties, to football game tailgate parties, food embodies the spirit of the celebration.

Fun. What would the elements of family, fellowship, and food be without the fun to join them all together? The preparation and the presentation are part of the fun — and the enjoyment of the total effort makes it all worthwhile!

Please join us as we celebrate the pleasures, the Simple Pleasures, of our lives.

Arab Mothers' Club
1998

The Arab Mothers' Club

The Arab Mothers' Club was formed in 1948 with a goal of helping mothers train and develop their children as better Christians. The club adopted Proverbs 22:6 as their motto: "Train up a child in the way he should go and when he is old he will not depart from it."

The Arab Mothers' Club quickly expanded their definition of 'children' to include all children in the community. The Arab Mothers' Club is involved in every aspect of our community and is committed to making the world a better place for all of our children. The club has been instrumental in building playgrounds and swimming pools, organizing girl scout troops, equipping libraries and recreation centers, teaching child care classes, and assisting with medical and dental needs. The proceeds from fund raising activities, including our annual fall Arts & Crafts Fair, are donated to the Arab Schools and other worthy organizations. All proceeds from the sale of this cookbook will be used to sponsor charitable projects in our community.

This cookbook celebrates the 50th anniversary of the founding of the Arab Mothers' Club. We dedicate it to the memory of our predecessors who established the vision for our children and our community that we strive to maintain.

Cookbook Committee

Co-Chairmen
Priscilla Bagwell
Patricia Elrod
Donna Taylor

Marketing Chairman: Dawn Morgan

Cookbook Marketing: Pam Cooper and Patti Hymer

Special Events Coordinator: Lisa Hart, Sherri King, Joy Privett

Finance and Distribution: Paula Moss, Toots Peterson, Cathy Strawn

Proofreading Chairman: Pam Hornsby

Correspondence Chairman: Cynthia Green

Publicity: Tawayna Vickers

Recipe Development: Tammy Anderson, Cynthia Green, Gail Lueker, Pat Martin, Paula Moss, Cheryl Nichols, Toots Peterson, Joy Privett, Linda Thompson, Andreé Tidmore

Contributors

Arab Mothers' Club gratefully acknowledges the following supporters of *Simple Pleasures* for their many and varied contributions. We realize that our ability to meet the needs of the children of Arab is enhanced by the generosity of the community.

Patrons

Amsouth Bank

Brindlee Mountain Telephone Company

Mr. and Mrs. Sid McDonald

Benefactors

Regions Bank

SouthTrust Bank

Syncro Corporation

Mr. and Mrs. Alan Bagwell

Mr. and Mrs. Jim Bobo

Mr. and Mrs. Bob Elrod

Mr. and Mrs. Gerald Jones

Mr. and Mrs. Randy Linn

Mr. and Mrs. Steve King

Mr. and Mrs. Brian Taylor

Supporters

Community Bank

Holloway and Hunt Insurance

Midas Burger

Mr. and Mrs. Bob Anderson

Mr. and Mrs. Max Carter

Mr. and Mrs. Frank Lee Cox

Mrs. Irby L. Elrod

Dr. and Mrs. Mike Freeman

Mr. Ralph Hammond

Mr. and Mrs. Joe Handschumacher

Dr. and Mrs. Robert Hargraves

Mr. and Mrs. Scotty Hawk

Mr. and Mrs. David Hill

Mrs. James Randolph Linn, Sr.

Mr. and Mrs. Doug Maze

Mr. and Mrs. Foster McDonald

Mrs. R.C. McGee

Mr. and Mrs. Jackie NeSmith

Mr. and Mrs. Ed Reed

About the Artist Nall

"I was born into an American W.A.S.P.'s nest on April 21, 1948. Along with Southern prejudice, hospitality and gentleness, I inherited artistic talent from my father. Twenty-two years later, in order to develop this talent, I ran away from home carrying a wife, a University of Alabama Art Degree, and a need to exorcise my desperation. Paris was my mistress, the Beaux Arts my new home. As Dali's disciple, androgeny and decadence expanded my mind. Inspired by his etchings and those of Dürer, Bellmer and J. Seraphim, I sat down to a linear feast — texture, image and symbol, and intricate transparencies. With astounding detail, the essence of my work through black and white pencil-painting was easily understood. The spontaneity, the aura, the sensuality of working from the model! Youth fed my vanities, while alcohol and drugs kept pushing me towards self destruction. Revealing oneself and living from one's art demanded courage, economy and hard work.

After seven years I moved to old Nice, the Riviera, to nature and light, a Mediterranean influence — and introspection; I fell in love and cleaned myself up. Watercolor obsessed me, and I was spoiled aesthetically, artistically — and adored it.

Through it all, work rewarded me, aided now by meditation, prayer and clean living. I bought Jean Dubuffet's studio in Vence, France, installed printing presses and began giving my own workshops. A four-year period in Mexican jungles refined my collage into mosaics. I paid homage with works called "New Orientalism," a doorway from east to west, memories of Venice and Istanbul.

I married again and with my wife Tuscia opened in Vence the N.A.L.L. (Nature Art & Life League) — a 17th Century farmhouse with eight buildings on 9 acres of terraced olive groves where artists live and work.

On the 5th of July 1997, my museum was inaugurated on the grounds, representing years of labor, travel and discovery."

PHOTO BY: HEIDI CHITWOOD

Nall with Mother, Mary Hollis, former Arab Mothers' Club member

About the Photographer

Ty first developed his passion for photography at age 15, when he received his first camera one Christmas from his parents, Ursula and Braxton Smith. With his new camera, he spent many weekends photographing his friends and the natural beauty of the Lynn's Dam area.

Ty is a 1981 graduate of Arab High School and received his bachelor of arts degree in commercial photography from the University of North Alabama. Ty and his wife, Jill, live in the Arab area, and they own and operate Photography by Ty in Guntersville, which is primarily a children's portrait studio with over 900 club members.

"It was a pleasure to be asked to do the photography for the Arab Mothers' Club Cookbook. I have personal ties to the club which my mother served as past president and was an active member from 1961–1969. I have fond memories of being at some of the events sponsored by the Mothers' Club."

Ty's studio, Photography by Ty, is located in beautiful downtown Guntersville, directly across the street from the courthouse square.

Special Thanks

We would like to thank NALL, Photography by Ty, and writer, Heidi Chitwood, whose talent has helped to make *Simple Pleasures* what it is. Their generous contribution has increased the quality of our book.

Our sincere thanks to Steve and Sherri King and Fine Things for providing the sets and props for our divider pages.

 Club Collect
(Since 1948)

Precious Father, give us hearts grateful for America and the American way of life; may we find joy in labor and love beauty in homes made glad with song.

In the laughter of little children, in songs of birds, in all "common things of life" help us to find thine ever present love.

May we learn to live wisely and well in the land which is ours, leaving it richer and more beautiful for having been our home.

Amen

Table of Contents

Arab Mothers' Club Spring Luncheon at Covington House

The turn of the century home of Reese and Julia Covington, owners and proprietors of the Covington House Restaurant in Guntersville, was one of the favorite settings for the annual Spring Luncheon of the Arab Mothers' Club. The elegant house served as a perfect backdrop for the elegant meal — as light and delicate as the soft spring breeze. These luscious recipes, each a trademark creation of Covington's at The Glover, will bring a touch of spring to your most special occasion.

Ham and Asparagus Crêpes

Curry-Artichoke Rice Salad

Cranberry-Apple Pear Casserole

Sunshine Salad

Rolls*

Cappuccino Meringues with Peppermint Ice Cream and Mocha Drizzle

Coffee With Friends

The children are at school, the beds are made, the dusting is finished. You have a few minutes of time for just you. Pamper yourself and a few of your close friends with a relaxing morning—a cozy time to visit and catch up on things. These easy-to-prepare treats will welcome friends and warm the soul. Bite-sized Orange Blossoms, served with chilled mimosas and your favorite brewed coffee, compliment savory sausage balls in apple butter. Relax and enjoy the morning...

Mimosas

Orange Blossoms

Strawberry Bread

Sausage Balls in Apple Butter

Assorted Fruit Tray with Fruit Dip*

Coffees*

*Recipes Not Included

Father's Day Grill

Honor the special men in your life with a celebration worthy of their fatherly heroics. What handy-man-turned-Little-League coach wouldn't love these flavorful grilled burgers, topped with bacon, BBQ sauce, and pineapples? Grandpa will enjoy the New Potato Salad even more than the standard version. And the whole family will adore the delicious Frozen Lime Torte on a hot June afternoon. Celebrate your family with this feast!

Grilled Pineapple Burgers

New Potato Salad

Broccoli Raisin Delight Salad

Frozen Lime Torte

Iced Tea or Favorite Beverages*

Summer Supper on the Back Porch

Extend the fun of a long summer day by enjoying a backyard barbeque with your neighbors. Have each friend bring a dish: salad with fresh garden greens, crusty piping-hot bread, trifle made with just-picked strawberries, frosty fruity tea. You just set a festive picnic table and grill these delicious spicy marinated shrimp. You and your party will be the hit of the neighborhood!

Barbequed Shrimp

Fresh Garden Salad*

Baked French Bread

Strawberry Trifle

Summer Iced Tea

Game Day

A traditional meal for a day of traditions — but there is always a surprise or two in store! Friends and family will enjoy the Artichoke Dip almost as much as the amazing run for a first down on 3rd-and-13! The dependable fried chicken and creamy potato salad will be as good and reliable as the quarterback. And that last-minute touchdown will ensure that your team's score equals the score your guests give to the rich Crème de Menthe Brownies.

Artichoke Dip with Tortilla Chips

Fried Chicken*

Creamy Potato Salad

Crowd Pleasing Cole Slaw

Rolls*

Crème de Menthe Brownies

Lemonade or Iced Tea*

Thanksgiving

We gather on this day to offer thanks for our family, friends, and food. Nothing is more special than the November feast we share with those most dear to us. This Thanksgiving table is filled with as many interesting additions as you have at your family gatherings: dressing with the warmth of hidden apples, the tartness of Sweet and Sour Green Beans, the creamy tang of Strawberry Pretzel Salad. The traditional Pecan Pie and the rich Pumpkin Roll, served with fresh coffee of course, are the perfect way to finish a day filled with traditions and riches!

Baked Turkey

Aunt Janie's Dressing

Sweet Potato Casserole

Corn Pudding

Strawberry Pretzel Salad

Squash Delight

Sweet and Sour Green Beans

Cinnamon Ring Pickles

Pumpkin Roll

Pecan Pie

Coffee*

Iced Tea*

Christmas Morning Brunch

After the excitement of a busy morning, your family is ready to relax and enjoy a day of building and sharing Christmas memories. A prepare-ahead brunch, with everybody's favorites, will allow time for eating and playing and visiting. Delicious Blueberry Muffins will fill little tummies, and hearty Sausage Breakfast Casserole and Garlic Cheese Grits will satisfy Santa's hungry helpers! And don't forget the special Christmas blessing to thank God for the greatest gift of all.

Sausage Breakfast Casserole

Garlic Cheese Grits

Curried Fruit

Blueberry Muffins

Coffee*

Appetizers and
Beverages

Christmas Punch

1 cup sugar
1 cup water
4 cups cranberry juice
1½ cups lemon juice
2 cups orange juice
2 cups pineapple juice
2 bottles ginger ale

Combine sugar and water in a small saucepan. Bring to a boil and stir until sugar is dissolved. Cover and reduce heat. Simmer over low heat for 5 minutes, without stirring. Remove from heat and combine with fruit juices. Chill thoroughly. Just before serving, pour over a block of ice in a punch bowl. Pour in ginger ale, ladle over ice until chilled and serve.

Fireside Coffee Mix

2 cups non-dairy coffee creamer
2 cups hot cocoa mix
1½ cups instant coffee
1½ cups sugar
1 teaspoon cinnamon
½ teaspoon nutmeg

Combine all ingredients and mix well. Store in a covered container. To serve, add 2 heaping tablespoons of mix to 1 cup boiling water.

Hot Punch

1 cup sugar
2½ cups water
1 (48-ounce) can pineapple juice
1 (42-ounce) can cranberry juice
2 sticks cinnamon
1½ teaspoons whole cloves
Pinch of salt

Combine sugar and water in a large saucepan. Bring to a boil, stirring, until sugar is dissolved. Add remaining ingredients and heat for 10 minutes.

The aroma of simmering spices will fill your whole house. Perfect on a cold winter evening.

Patsy's Slush Punch

5 cups sugar
2 packages powdered drink mix (any flavor)
1 package lemon powdered drink mix
1 (46-ounce) can pineapple juice
1½ gallons water
1 (2-liter) bottle lemon-lime soda

Dissolve sugar and powdered drink mix in juice in a 2-gallon container. Add water and stir to combine. Freeze. Four to six hours before serving, remove from freezer and thaw. When ready to serve, break up with a potato masher and pour into a punch bowl. Add soda, stir and serve.

"Life is made up, not of great sacrifices or duties, but of little things, in which smiles and kindnesses and small obligations win and preserve the heart."
—Humphrey Davy

Peach Nectar Punch

1 (6-ounce) can frozen orange juice concentrate
1 quart peach nectar
1 quart ginger ale
1 quart frozen peach slices

Combine juice, nectar and ginger ale in a punch bowl. Float peach slices in punch and serve.

Yield: 17 servings.

Refreshing Fruit Tea

3 cups boiling water
4 tea bags
¾ cup sugar
4 cups cold water
1 cup orange juice
1 cup pineapple juice
¼ cup lemon juice

Pour boiling water over tea bags, cover and steep 5 minutes. Remove and discard tea bags. Stir in sugar until dissolved. Add cold water and juices. Serve over ice.

Banana Breakfast Shake

1½ cups skim or 1% milk
1   peeled and sliced medium
    banana, frozen
½   teaspoon vanilla, optional
¼   teaspoon almond extract,
    optional
Cinnamon, optional

Combine all ingredients except cinnamon in a blender. Blend until smooth, about 20 seconds. Pour into glasses and sprinkle with cinnamon, if desired.

Yield: 2 servings.

To freeze bananas, wrap slices in plastic wrap or place in a freezer bag. Freeze several hours or overnight.

Banana Slush

1   (6-ounce) can frozen orange
    juice concentrate, thawed
1   (6-ounce) can frozen
    lemonade concentrate,
    thawed
3   bananas, mashed
2   cups sugar
2   quarts water
1   quart lemon-lime soda

Combine juices, bananas, sugar and water in a 1-gallon container. Freeze until solid, stirring occasionally. To serve, thaw to a slush and add soda.

Christmas Wassail

1   gallon apple cider
1   quart orange juice
1   cup lemon juice
1   quart sweetened pineapple
    juice
1   cup sugar
4   cinnamon sticks
24 whole cloves

Combine all ingredients in a large saucepan or coffee urn. Heat thoroughly and serve hot. Garnish with additional cinnamon sticks, if desired.

Yield: 20 servings.

Spicy Perk-a-Punch

2   quarts cranberry juice
     cocktail
2   quarts unsweetened
     pineapple juice
I   quart water
⅔   cup firmly packed brown
     sugar
I   tablespoon whole cloves
I   tablespoon whole allspice
4   cinnamon sticks
2   lemons, quartered

Combine fruit juice and water in a 30-cup electric percolator. Place remaining ingredients in basket and perk for 30 minutes.

Yield: 30 servings.

Summer Iced Tea

6   tea bags
4   cups boiling water
I½ cups sugar
I   (6-ounce) can frozen
     lemonade concentrate,
     thawed
I   (6-ounce) can frozen orange
     juice concentrate, thawed
10   cups water

Steep tea bags in boiling water for 5 minutes. Discard tea bags and add remaining ingredients. Serve over ice.

Variation: Add I cup pineapple juice and garnish with a sprig of fresh mint.

Yield: I gallon.

Mimosas

I   (12-ounce) can frozen
     orange juice concentrate
¼   cup plus 2 tablespoons
     orange-flavored liqueur
I   (750-ml.) bottle champagne,
     chilled

Prepare orange juice according to directions. Stir in liqueur, cover and chill thoroughly. Stir in champagne just before serving.

Homemade Coffee Liqueur

2   cups water
4   cups sugar
1   (2-ounce) jar instant coffee
2   vanilla beans
1   pint brandy

Bring water to a boil in a saucepan. Add sugar and coffee and stir until dissolved. Add vanilla bean and brandy. Remove from heat and cool until room temperature. Pour into a glass container, cover and let stand at room temperature for at least 30 days. The longer it stands, the better it gets.

Makes wonderful Christmas gifts.

Citrus Punch

3   envelopes dry Tom Collins
    mix
2   tablespoons sugar
1   (2-liter) bottle lemon-lime
    soda
1   pint gin
3   lemons, sliced
4-5 oranges, sliced
½   bottle cherries, with juice
Lemon-lime soda

Dissolve drink mix and sugar in soda. Add gin and fruit and chill. When ready to serve, mix with equal parts lemon-lime soda.

Punchy Sangria

2   (6-ounce) cans frozen pink
    lemonade concentrate,
    thawed
4½ cups Rosé wine, chilled
Juice of 1 lime
2   cups club soda, chilled
1   lemon, thinly sliced
1   orange, thinly sliced

Combine lemonade concentrate, wine and lime juice. Stir until well blended. Slowly stir in club soda. Add fruit slices and chill until ready to serve.

Looks very festive served in a clear glass pitcher.

Rosy Wassail

1   pint cranberry juice cocktail
1   (6-ounce) can frozen orange
    juice concentrate, thawed
2   cups water
1   tablespoon sugar
1/4 teaspoon allspice
3 1/2 cups white wine
Few drops red food coloring,
    optional
Orange slices
Whole cloves

Combine juices, water, sugar and allspice in a large kettle. Bring to a simmer, add wine and heat through. Do not boil. Add food coloring if desired. Pour into a preheated punch bowl. Stud orange slices with cloves and float on top of punch.

Yield: 12 to 14 servings.

Holiday Spiced Tea

2   (26-ounce) jars instant
    orange drink mix
1   (3-ounce) jar instant tea
2   (8 1/2-ounce) packages red hot
    candy
1   (6-ounce) package
    sweetened lemonade mix
1   cup sugar
2   teaspoons cinnamon
2   teaspoons nutmeg
2   teaspoons ground cloves
2   teaspoons allspice

Combine all ingredients in a large bowl. Store in an airtight container. To serve place 1 tablespoon mix in a large cup and add boiling water.

Makes a great party favor - fill small jars with mix and decorate with pretty ribbons.

"Tea, thou soft, thou sober, sage and venerable drink..."
                      -Colley Cibber

Artichoke Dip

1 cup sour cream
1 cup mayonnaise
1 cup grated Parmesan cheese
1 small jar marinated artichoke hearts, drained and chopped
1 small onion, chopped

Combine sour cream, mayonnaise and Parmesan. Stir in artichoke hearts and onion. Pour into a 1-quart baking dish and bake in preheated 375° oven for 30 minutes. Serve with thinly sliced French bread or bagel chips.

Broccoli Dip

2 packages frozen chopped broccoli
1 large onion, chopped
½ cup margarine
2 cans cream of mushroom soup
2 rolls garlic cheese, sliced
1 (8-ounce) can mushroom pieces, drained
Dip-style corn chips

Cook broccoli according to package directions, drain and set aside. Sauté onion in butter until translucent. Add soup and cheese. Simmer, stirring, until cheese is melted. Add mushrooms and broccoli and heat through. Serve with corn chips.

Hawaiian Cheese Dip

1½ cups sour cream
1 (8-ounce) package cream cheese, softened
2 cups shredded pasteurized process cheese
1 small can mild green chilies, drained
½ cup minced ham
2 small green onions, minced
Dash of Worcestershire sauce
1 round loaf Hawaiian bread

Combine all ingredients except bread in a large bowl. Slice top from bread and hollow out insides, leaving a ½-inch shell. Reserve bread crumbs for another use. Spoon cheese mixture into bread shell and replace top. Wrap in foil and bake in a preheated 350° oven for 1 hour. Serve with dip-style corn chips.

Tex-Mex Dip

1   can bean dip
1   package taco seasoning mix
12 ounces sour cream
Shredded mild Cheddar cheese
1   small can sliced black olives,
    drained
1   medium tomato, chopped
3   green onions, chopped
Tortilla chips

Spread bean dip on a large platter. Combine taco seasoning and sour cream and spread over bean dip. Sprinkle with cheese, tomatoes, black olives and onions. Serve with tortilla chips.

Hot Crab Dip

2   (8-ounce) packages cream
    cheese, softened
1   (10-ounce) can crab meat,
    rinsed and drained
¼   cup mayonnaise
½   cup sour cream
¼   teaspoon garlic powder
2   teaspoons dry mustard
1½ tablespoons white wine
2⅓ teaspoons powdered sugar
2   teaspoons onion juice
Salt to taste

Freezes well. Thaw slightly before heating.

Combine all ingredients in top of a double boiler and heat, stirring, until smooth. Turn into a baking dish and place in a preheated 350° oven. Bake until bubbly. Serve hot with crackers.

Shrimp and Artichoke Dip

1   (16-ounce) jar artichoke
    hearts, drained and chopped
1   cup mayonnaise
1   cup grated Parmesan cheese
1   cup cooked, chopped shrimp
½   can water chestnuts, drained
    and chopped

Combine all ingredients and spoon into a greased baking dish. Bake in a preheated 350° oven until hot, about 25 minutes. Serve with crackers.

Judy's Beef Dip

1 (8-ounce) package cream
  cheese, softened
2 tablespoons milk
1½ teaspoons minced onion
½ teaspoon garlic powder
1 (2½-ounce) jar dried beef,
  chopped
8 ounces sour cream
Chopped pecans
Whole wheat wafers

Combine all ingredients except pecans and crackers. Place in a baking dish and top with pecans. Bake in a preheated 325° oven until hot, about 15 minutes. Serve with crackers.

Corn Dip

1 (8-ounce) package cream
  cheese, softened
2 tablespoons mayonnaise
1 can Mexican-style corn, drained
1 cup grated cheese

Combine cream cheese and mayonnaise. Add corn and cheese and mix thoroughly. Serve with corn chips.

Vegetable Spread

2 tomatoes, finely chopped
1 cup chopped celery
1 small onion, minced
1 green bell pepper, minced
1 cucumber, minced
1 envelope unflavored gelatin
¼ cup cold water
¼ cup boiling water
1 pint mayonnaise
1 teaspoon salt

Variation: Stuff into a tomato for a light summer lunch.

Drain vegetables well on paper towels. Soften gelatin in cold water. Add boiling water and cool. Fold in mayonnaise and salt and add vegetables. Cover and chill. Use as a spread or dip on bread, crackers or chips.

Texas Caviar

2   cans tiny black-eyed peas, drained
2   cans white shoe peg corn, drained
1   bunch parsley, chopped
1   bunch green onions, chopped
1   large green bell pepper, chopped
1   teaspoon minced garlic
2-3 tomatoes, chopped
1   large bottle zesty Italian dressing
1   small can jalapeño peppers, drained and chopped
Nacho chips

Combine all ingredients except chips in a large bowl. Cover and chill at least for 2 hours before serving. Serve with chips.

Yield: 10 servings.

Shrimp `Wonderful`

2   pounds shrimp, cooked in shells
3   tablespoons butter
2   cups grated Swiss cheese
2   cups grated mild Cheddar cheese
½   cup heavy cream
2   eggs, lightly beaten
½   cup dry white wine
1   teaspoon dry mustard
1   teaspoon Worcestershire sauce
Salt and pepper to taste
Small pastry shells or toast points

Variation: Substitute chopped cooked chicken or ham for the shrimp.

Peel and devein shrimp. Leave whole if small and cut in half if large. Set aside. Melt butter in a saucepan and stir in cheeses. Heat, stirring, until cheese is melted. Add cream, eggs, wine, mustard, Worcestershire, and salt and pepper to taste. Cook over low heat, stirring, until mixture is thickened. Add shrimp and heat thoroughly. Serve in pastry shells or over toast points.

Yield: 6 servings.

Ugly Dip

1 large onion, chopped
2 large tomatoes, chopped
3 ounces sliced jalapeño
  peppers, chopped
3-4 stalks celery, chopped
2 cans black olives, drained
  and chopped
3 tablespoons vinegar
1 tablespoon olive oil
Garlic salt
Salt and pepper

Combine onion, tomato, jalapeño, celery and olives in a large bowl. Toss with vinegar and olive oil and season to taste with garlic salt, salt and pepper. Serve with dip-style corn chips or tortilla chips.

Dill Dip

⅔ cup sour cream
⅔ cup mayonnaise
1 teaspoon seasoned salt
1 teaspoon onion flakes
2 teaspoons chopped fresh dill
3 drops hot pepper sauce
½ teaspoon Worcestershire sauce
1 teaspoon Accent seasoning
1 tablespoon chopped parsley

Combine all ingredients and mix well. Cover and refrigerate overnight. Serve with raw vegetables or chips.

This is also wonderful on baked potatoes.

Green Goddess Dip

2 (3-ounce) packages cream
  cheese, softened
1 cup mayonnaise
1 cup sour cream
2 tablespoons lemon juice
1½ tablespoons tarragon vinegar
1 teaspoon garlic salt
½ cup chopped green onions,
  including tops
⅔ cup chopped parsley

Combine all ingredients and mix well. Cover and refrigerate overnight. Serve with raw vegetables or chips.

Artichoke Squares

1	onion, chopped
1	teaspoon minced garlic
2	tablespoons margarine or butter
4	eggs, lightly beaten
¼	cup cracker crumbs

Salt and pepper

½	teaspoon oregano
½	teaspoon lemon juice
½	teaspoon hot pepper sauce
8	ounces shredded sharp Cheddar cheese
2	jars marinated artichoke hearts, drained and chopped

Sauté onions and garlic in butter until transparent. Remove from heat and cool. Combine eggs, cracker crumbs, salt, pepper, oregano, lemon juice, cheese, hot pepper sauce and parsley. Add onion mixture and blend. Add artichokes and mix thoroughly. Spread in a greased 9 x 13-inch pan and bake in a preheated 350° oven for 30 minutes. Cut into bite-size squares to serve.

May be frozen after cooking.

Stuffed Mushrooms

1	(1-quart) package large mushrooms

2-3 green onions, chopped
Butter

1	(3-ounce) can crab or shrimp pieces, rinsed and drained

Grated Parmesan cheese
Few drops of hot pepper sauce
Bread crumbs

Remove stems from mushrooms and chop. Sauté with green onions in butter until limp. Add crab or shrimp, Parmesan and hot pepper sauce. Add enough bread crumbs to stiffen to a stuffing consistency. Place mushroom caps in a greased casserole and stuff with bread crumb mixture. Cover and bake in a preheated 325° oven for 25 minutes.

"The test of pleasure is the memory it brings."

—Jean-Paul Richter

Caramel Dip

1 (6-ounce) package
   butterscotch morsels
1 can sweetened condensed milk
½ teaspoon salt
½ teaspoon cinnamon
1½ tablespoons white vinegar
Granny Smith apples, cut into
   wedges and soaked in a
   mixture of water and ¼ cup
   salt for 30 minutes

Pour milk over morsels, without mixing. Microwave on high for 3 minutes. Stir and add remaining ingredients except apples. Microwave on high for 2 more minutes and stir until smooth. Rinse and drain apple wedges and serve with dip.

Chicken Log

2 (8-ounce) packages cream
   cheese, softened
1 tablespoon steak sauce
½ teaspoon curry powder
1½ cups minced cooked chicken
   (2 to 3 breasts)
⅓ cup minced celery
Chopped pecans

Combine cream cheese, steak sauce and curry powder. Blend well. Mix in chicken and celery, roll into a log, cover and refrigerate. Roll in pecans and serve with assorted crackers.

Cheese Cookies

8 ounces grated sharp Cheddar
   cheese
2 cups flour
1 cup margarine
¼ teaspoon cayenne pepper
¼ teaspoon salt
2 cups crispy rice cereal

Combine all ingredients except cereal and knead together until well blended. Add cereal and work together. Drop by teaspoonfuls onto an ungreased baking sheet. Bake in a preheated 325° oven until done, about 20 minutes.

Yield: 4½ to 5 dozen cookies.

Ginger Chicken Bacon Bites

12 ounces boneless, skinless chicken breasts
¼ cup orange marmalade
2 tablespoons soy sauce
¼ teaspoon ground ginger
⅛ teaspoon garlic powder
12 slices bacon
1 (8-ounce) can whole water chestnuts, drained and halved

Cut chicken into 24 bite-size pieces. Set aside. Combine marmalade, soy sauce, ginger and garlic powder in a medium mixing bowl. Add chicken pieces, toss to coat, cover and chill 30 minutes. Arrange bacon slices on a broiler pan. Broil 4 to 5 inches from heat for 1 to 2 minutes, or until partially cooked, but not crisp. Drain off fat. Cool bacon and cut in half crosswise. Drain chicken. Wrap a slice of bacon around each chicken piece and a chestnut half. Secure with a wooden pick and place on cooled broiler rack. Broil 4 to 5 inches from heat for 3 to 5 minutes, or until chicken is cooked, turning once.

Yield: 2 dozen.

Nalls Finger Potatoes

1-1½ inch diameter potatoes, 8 count per person
Big cooking salt
Mint (bunch)
Olive oil
Cloves (optional)

Boil potatoes in water with mint and cloves until soft. Leave skins on. Once drained and still warm, add olive oil. Pour on generously and sprinkle large cooking salt over potatoes. Decorate with a few twigs of fresh mint.

Good hot, room temperature or cold. As good as an hors d'oeuvre or as a side dish. Eat with your fingers. A good replacement for potato chips and dip (ugh!).

Holiday Cheese Ball

1　(6-ounce) package blue cheese, softened
2　(5-ounce) jars Old English cheese
2　(8-ounce) packages cream cheese, softened
1　tablespoon finely chopped onion
1　tablespoon Worcestershire sauce
½　cup chopped parsley, divided
1　cup chopped nuts

Combine cheeses. Add onion, Worcestershire sauce and half of parsley. Form into a ball and roll in nuts and remaining parsley. Chill until firm. Serve with crackers.

Pineapple Cheese Ball

2　(8-ounce) packages cream cheese, softened
1　(8-ounce) can crushed pineapple, drained
2　cups chopped pecans, divided
¼　cup finely chopped green bell pepper
2　tablespoons finely chopped onion
1　tablespoon seasoned salt

Beat cream cheese with a fork until smooth. Stir in pineapple, 1 cup pecans, bell pepper, onion and salt. Shape into a ball and roll in remaining pecans. Wrap and refrigerate until firm. Serve with crisp crackers.

Oyster Ball

2　(8-ounce) packages cream cheese, softened
2-3 tablespoons mayonnaise
2　teaspoons Worcestershire sauce
1　large clove garlic, pressed
½　small onion, finely chopped
2　cans smoked oysters, drained and chopped
⅛　teaspoon salt
½　cup finely chopped pecans

Combine cream cheese with enough mayonnaise to make smooth. Add Worcestershire sauce, onion and garlic. Combine well. Mix in oysters, cover and refrigerate for 2 hours. Form into a ball and roll in pecans. Chill until ready to serve. Serve with crackers and cocktail sauce.

Spicy Cheese Ball

2 (8-ounce) packages cream
cheese, softened
2 cups shredded sharp
Cheddar cheese
1 tablespoon chopped pimento
1 tablespoon chopped onion
1 tablespoon chopped green
bell pepper
1 tablespoon Worcestershire
sauce
1 teaspoon lemon juice
1/4 teaspoon garlic salt
Dash of cayenne pepper
Salt to taste
Finely chopped pecans

Place cheeses in a bowl and mix until well blended. Add remaining ingredients except pecans and mix well. Cover and chill for several hours. Shape into a ball and roll in pecans. Chill until serving time. Serve with crackers.

Coastal Crab Dip

8 ounces fresh crab meat,
drained and picked clean
1 cup sour cream
3 tablespoons chili sauce
1/4 cup minced green onions
3 tablespoons minced celery
1 tablespoon lemon juice
2 teaspoons prepared horseradish
1/8 teaspoon white pepper

**Light or fat-free sour cream
may be used.**

Flake crab meat. Combine remaining ingredients and mix well. Stir in crab meat, cover and chill for several hours. Serve with assorted crackers.

Yield: 2 cups.

"Eating is heaven."
—Korean proverb

Crab Mousse

1   can cream of mushroom soup
2   (3-ounce) packages cream
     cheese, softened
1   cup mayonnaise
1   tablespoon Worcestershire
     sauce
1½ envelopes unflavored gelatin
¼   cup cold water
1   (6½-ounce) can crab meat,
     rinsed and drained
1   cup finely chopped celery
1   small onion, grated
Chopped green bell pepper or
     pimento, optional

*Variation: For Shrimp Mousse,
substitute tomato soup and
shrimp for cream of mushroom
soup and crab.*

Combine soup, cream cheese, mayonnaise and Worcestershire sauce in top of a double boiler. Simmer, stirring, until cheese is melted. Combine gelatin and water in a small dish. Let stand until thickened. Stir into soup mixture. Cool mixture and add remaining ingredients. Pour into an oiled seafood mold and chill until firm. Turn out onto a serving platter and serve with crackers.

Shrimp Dip

½   cup cooked shrimp, finely
     ground
1   cup sour cream
¼   cup chili sauce
2   teaspoons lemon juice
½   teaspoon salt
⅛   teaspoon pepper
1   teaspoon prepared
     horseradish
Dash of hot pepper sauce

Combine all ingredients and blend well. Cover and refrigerate until chilled. Serve with chips.

Yield: 1½ cups.

*"Anticipate the good so that
you may enjoy it."*
—Ethiopian proverb

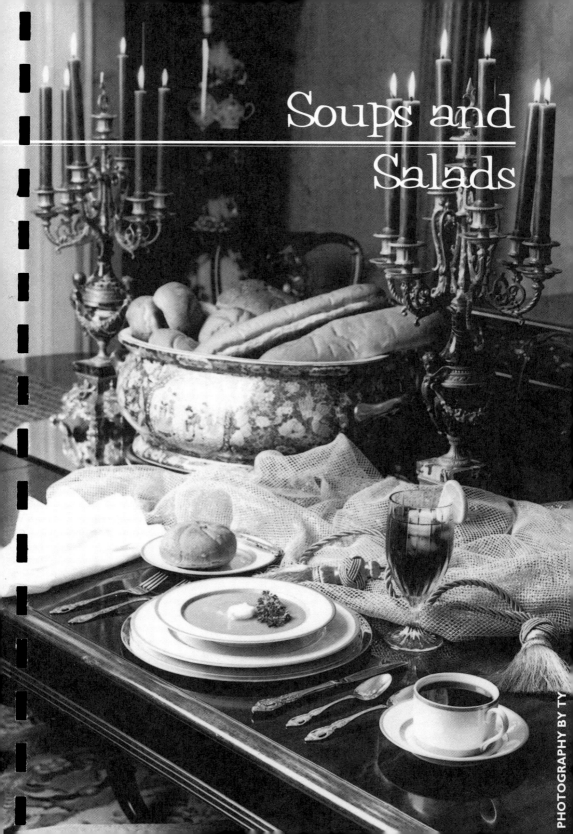

Soups and Salads

Cold Pea Soup with Mint

1 (10-ounce) package frozen tiny peas
1 medium onion, thinly sliced
1 tablespoon minced fresh mint
3 cups chicken stock, divided
2 tablespoons flour
½ cup heavy cream
Salt and pepper
Sour cream
Mint sprigs

A refreshing, make-ahead soup for a hot summer day.

Cook peas and onion in 1 cup water until very tender. Add mint and purée in blender until smooth. Set aside. Place ½ cup stock and the flour in a saucepan and blend until smooth. Add remaining stock and cook, stirring, until thickened. Add pea mixture and bring to a boil. Stir in cream and salt and pepper to taste. Remove from heat, cover and chill thoroughly.

To serve, ladle soup into chilled serving bowls and garnish with a dollop of sour cream and a sprig of mint.

Yield: 4 servings.

Taco Soup

1 pound ground round beef
1 large onion, chopped
1 package original Ranch dressing mix
1 package taco seasoning
2 (16-ounce) cans pinto beans, drained
1 can whole kernel corn, drained
1 can diced tomatoes
1 can tomatoes and green chilies
1 quart tomato juice

Cook ground beef and onion in a large saucepan until beef is browned. Drain well and add remaining ingredients. Cook, stirring occasionally, until heated through. Garnish with tortilla chips and sour cream.

"To affect the quality of the day; that is the art of life."
—Henry David Thoreau

Homemade Chicken Soup

I	(4-pound) fryer
I	bunch celery, sliced
I	quart tomatoes, chopped
I	(I-pound) bag frozen vegetable gumbo mixture
I	can diced tomatoes and green chilies
I	large onion, diced
½	cup dried chives
4	chicken bouillon cubes

Salt and pepper to taste

Boil chicken until cooked and tender. Remove from broth and set broth aside. When chicken is cool enough to handle, debone and dice. Return chicken to broth, add remaining ingredients and simmer for I hour. Serve with corn bread or crackers.

Leftovers may be frozen.

Chicken Brunswick Stew – Slow-Cooker Style

2	large onions, chopped
6	skinless, boneless chicken breasts
2	(15-ounce) cans cream-style corn
I	(28-ounce) can crushed tomatoes
I	(12-ounce) bottle chili sauce
I	(14½-ounce) can chicken broth
¼	cup Worcestershire sauce
¼	cup butter or margarine, sliced
2	tablespoons cider vinegar
2	teaspoons dry mustard
½	teaspoon salt
½	teaspoon pepper
½	teaspoon hot pepper sauce, or to taste

Layer onion in bottom of a 4-quart slow cooker. Top with chicken breasts. Add remaining ingredients, cover and cook on high until chicken is tender, about 4 hours. Remove chicken, shred and return to stew.

Great for a busy day.

Yield: 4 quarts.

Chicken and Rice Soup

4	large chicken breasts or I whole chicken, skinned
4 or 5	medium potatoes, peeled and diced
I	large onion, diced
I	(10-ounce) package yellow saffron rice

Place chicken in a large saucepan and cover with water. Bring to a boil, reduce heat and simmer until chicken is tender, about 40 to 50 minutes. Remove from broth and let cool. Add potatoes and onion to broth and boil for a few minutes. Stir in rice. When chicken is cool enough to handle, debone and shred. Return to broth and add enough water to fill saucepan. Bring to a boil, reduce heat, cover and simmer until potatoes are tender.

Grandmother's Chicken Soup

4	boneless chicken breasts
2	tablespoons butter
2	chicken bouillon cubes
4 or 5	potatoes, peeled and diced
I	medium onion, chopped
I	can English peas
I	small can tomato sauce

Salt and pepper to taste

Combine chicken, butter and bouillon cubes in a 4-quart pressure cooker. Cover with water and cook 10 to 15 minutes. Remove to a large saucepan and add remaining ingredients. Cover with water and cook until potatoes are done.

Yield: 5 servings.

Onion Soup

4	(¾-inch) slices French bread
6	tablespoons butter, divided
6	large onions, sliced
6	cups beef stock
I	tablespoon flour
I	cup grated Parmesan cheese

Spread bread with 2 tablespoons butter. Toast until brown and set aside. Melt remaining butter in a stock pot. Add onions and sauté until tender. Add stock and salt and pepper to taste. Stir in flour and mix until smooth. Bring to a boil, reduce heat and simmer 15 minutes. Ladle into individual serving bowls and place a slice of bread on top of each serving. Sprinkle with cheese and broil until light brown.

Yield: 4 servings.

Chili

1	pound boneless chuck roast, cut into 1/4-inch cubes
1	pound lean ground beef
1	pound spicy pork sausage
1 1/2	cups chopped onion
1 1/2	cups chopped green bell pepper
2	tablespoons minced garlic
1	zucchini, chopped
2	fresh jalapeño peppers, seeded and finely chopped
1/4	cup plus 1 tablespoon chili powder
1	teaspoon salt
2 1/2	teaspoons ground cumin
2	teaspoons cocoa
1/4	teaspoon pepper
2	bay leaves
2	(10-ounce) cans beef broth, undiluted
2	(16-ounce) cans Italian-style tomatoes, drained and chopped
1	(16-ounce) can tomato sauce
1	(6-ounce) can tomato paste
1	(16-ounce) can red kidney beans, drained
1	cup beer

Sour cream
Chopped green onion

Sauté meats in a large stock pot over medium heat, stirring often, until brown. Remove meat from pot with a slotted spoon and drain well. Sauté onion, bell pepper, garlic and zucchini in drippings until tender. Drain drippings. Return meat to pot and add jalapeño, chili powder, salt, cumin, cocoa, pepper and bay leaves. Stir until well blended. Add broth, tomatoes, tomato sauce and tomato paste. Stir well. Bring to a boil, reduce heat and simmer, uncovered until mixture thickens, about 25 minutes. Add beans and simmer an additional 20 minutes. Stir in beer and simmer 15 more minutes, stirring often. Serve garnished with a dollop of sour cream and a sprinkling of green onion.

Yield: 3 quarts.

Four Hour Beef Stew

1 1/2	pounds stew meat
	Salt and pepper
4	potatoes, diced
3	carrots, sliced
1	stalk celery, chopped
1	medium onion, chopped
1	can golden mushroom soup

Place meat in bottom of a 3-quart casserole. Salt and pepper to taste. Top with layers of carrots, onions, celery and potatoes. Spread with soup. Cover tightly with foil and bake in a preheated 275° oven until meat is tender, 4 to 5 hours.

Yield: 6 to 8 servings.

Oyster Stew

1 pint oysters
1½ tablespoons all-purpose flour
1½ teaspoons salt
2 tablespoons water
2 tablespoons butter or
  margarine
1 small onion, chopped and
  sautéed
3 cups milk, scalded
1 cup whipping cream, scalded

Drain oysters and reserve liquid. Combine reserved liquid, flour, salt and water in a saucepan. Bring to a boil, reduce heat and stir until smooth. Add oysters, butter and sautéed onions. Simmer until edges of oysters curl, about 5 minutes. Stir in milk and cream. Cover and remove from heat. Let stand 15 minutes before serving.

Reheat any leftovers over very low heat.

Yield: 4 to 6 servings.

Baked Potato Soup

⅔ cup butter or margarine
⅔ cup all-purpose flour
7 cups milk
4 large baking potatoes,
  cooked, peeled and cubed
4 green onions, sliced
12 strips bacon, cooked crisp
  and crumbled
1¼ cups shredded Cheddar
  cheese
8 ounces sour cream
¾ teaspoon salt
½ teaspoon pepper

Melt butter in a large soup kettle or Dutch oven. Stir in flour and cook over low heat until smooth. Gradually add milk, and cook, stirring constantly, until thickened. Add potatoes and onions. Bring to a boil, stirring constantly. Reduce heat and simmer 10 minutes. Add remaining ingredients and stir until cheese is melted. Serve immediately.

Yield: 8 to 10 servings.

"It isn't the great big pleasures that count the most, it's making a great deal out of the little ones."
                    —Jean Webster

Potato Soup

6 large baking potatoes, peeled and diced
2 stalks celery, chopped
2 carrots, sliced
1 onion, chopped
1 can cream of chicken soup
½ cup margarine
1 (8-ounce) package cream cheese
2 cups milk
Water
Bacon bits
Grated cheese
Chopped green onions

Place potatoes, celery, carrots and onion in a large pot. Cover with water and cook until potatoes are tender. Drain. Add remaining ingredients and stir thoroughly. Bring to a boil, reduce heat and simmer slowly for 30 to 45 minutes, stirring frequently. Serve garnished with bacon bits, cheese and green onion.

Yield 10 servings.

"The ordinary arts we practice every day at home are of more importance to the soul than their simplicity might suggest."
—Thomas Moore

Broccoli Cheese Soup

1 can cream of celery soup
2 cans broccoli soup
2 cans potato soup
1 can Cheddar cheese soup
2 cans chunk-style ham, chopped
1 (10-ounce) package chopped broccoli
1 can julienne carrots
2 cans evaporated milk
1 pint half and half

Combine all ingredients in a large crock pot and heat until thoroughly heated and broccoli is cooked.

Minnesota Wild Rice Soup

3 ounces wild rice
1 teaspoon oil
4 cups water
1 medium onion, chopped
6 tablespoons butter
10 tablespoons flour
3 cups chicken stock
2 cups half and half or milk
Salt and pepper to taste

May be made a day ahead and reheated before serving.

Sauté rice in oil until lightly toasted. Add water and bring to a boil. Cook until rice begins to pop open. Do not overcook. Drain and reserve 1½ cups water from rice. Melt butter and sauté onion until transparent. Add flour and mix until smooth. Cook over low heat until thickened. Do not brown. Gradually add reserved rice water and chicken stock, stirring constantly. Cook, stirring, over medium heat until mixture comes to a boil. Add rice and half and half. Reduce heat and simmer 20 minutes. Do not allow it to boil.

Our Favorite Tortilla Soup

1 cup chopped onion
4 cloves garlic, minced
3 Anaheim chili peppers, seeded and minced
1 tablespoon cumin seed
2 tablespoons cooking oil
1½ cups fresh-cut corn kernels (3 ears)
3 medium tomatoes, chopped
2 (14½-ounce) cans reduced sodium chicken broth
1½ cups cooked, coarsely shredded chicken
½ cup snipped cilantro
Crushed tortilla chips
Shredded cheese
Lime wedges
Fresh cilantro sprigs

Sauté onion, garlic, peppers and cumin seed in hot oil in a large pot until tender, stirring constantly. Add corn, tomatoes, chicken broth, chicken and cilantro. Bring to a boil. Reduce heat and simmer, covered, for 10 minutes. To serve, divide tortilla chips among serving bowls. Ladle soup over chips and garnish with remaining ingredients.

Yield: 6 servings.

Portuguese Red Bean Soup

1   pound dried kidney beans
Ham bone
3   potatoes, diced
2   onions, sliced and sautéed
1   tablespoon vinegar
1   teaspoon paprika
1   teaspoon salt
1   teaspoon pepper
1   teaspoon thyme
1   small can tomato paste
2   Italian sausages, diced

Rinse beans and place in a large stock pot. Cover with water and boil for 1 hour. Add remaining ingredients and additional water to cover. Bring to a boil, reduce heat and simmer 6 hours, stirring occasionally. Check and adjust seasonings after 3 hours.

This is a wonderfully hearty soup that warms the soul on a chilly night. Serve with a grilled pimento cheese sandwich.

Yield: 10 servings.

Cuban Black Bean Soup

1   pound dried black beans
2   quarts water
2   tablespoons salt
1   ham bone
5   cloves garlic, peeled
1½ tablespoons cumin
1½ tablespoons oregano
1   ounce white wine vinegar
1½ pounds onions, finely
    chopped
1½ pound green bell peppers,
    finely chopped
5   ounces Spanish oil
Chopped green onions
Sour cream
Grated sharp cheese

Soak beans in water overnight. Drain and rinse. Place in a large stock pot and add 2 quarts water, salt and ham bone. Bring to a boil and cook until beans are soft. Place garlic, cumin and oregano in a food processor and process until crushed. Add vinegar and process briefly. Sauté onions and peppers in hot oil until onions are brown. Add garlic mixture, reduce heat and continue cooking. Add bean mixture and cook 1½ to 2 hours. Serve with rice and garnish with green onions, sour cream and cheese.

Yield: 6 servings.

Spicy Black-Eyed Pea Soup

1	pound mild or hot pork sausage
1	cup chopped celery
1	cup chopped green bell pepper
1	cup chopped onion
2	(15-ounce) cans jalapeño or regular black-eyed peas
1	can shoe peg corn
2	cans tomatoes with green chilies
1	package frozen okra, unbreaded

Salt and pepper to taste

Brown sausage and drain. Add chopped vegetables and sauté until tender. Add remaining ingredients and bring to a boil. Reduce, cover and simmer until okra is tender, about 30 minutes.

Yield: 10 to 12 servings.

Perfect for New Year's Day.

"Whatever the seasoning, whatever the dish, whatever the occasion, do it generously and with love, for that in the end is what the shared experience of cooking and eating is all about."
—Elizabeth Rozin

Spinach and Strawberry Salad

Fresh spinach, washed and dried
Fresh strawberries, sliced

½	cup sugar
2	tablespoons sesame seeds
1	tablespoon poppy seeds
1½	teaspoons minced onion
1	teaspoon Worcestershire sauce
1½	teaspoons paprika
½	cup vegetable oil
¼	teaspoon cider vinegar

Place spinach and strawberries in a salad bowl. Combine remaining ingredients in a covered container and shake to blend. When ready to serve, pour over salad and toss to coat.

Colorful and delicious.

Minted Melon Summer Salad

1 cup water
¾ cup sugar
3 tablespoons lime juice
1½ teaspoons chopped fresh
   mint
¾ teaspoon anise seed
Pinch of salt
5 cups cubed watermelon
3 cups cubed cantaloupe
3 cups cubed honeydew melon
2 cups peach slices
1 cup fresh blueberries

A summertime treat - the colorful fruit and unique dressing make this refreshing salad irresistible.

Combine water, sugar, lime juice, mint, anise and salt in a small saucepan. Bring to a boil and boil for 2 minutes. Remove from heat. Cover and cool completely. Place fruit in a large bowl, add syrup and stir gently to coat. Cover and chill for at least 2 hours, stirring occasionally. Drain before serving in a glass container or melon boat.

Yield: 12 to 14 servings.

Corn Salad

2 (12-ounce) cans shoe peg
   corn, drained
2 tomatoes, unpeeled, seeded
   and chopped
1 purple onion, chopped
1 green bell pepper, chopped
1 cucumber, peeled, seeded
   and chopped
½ cup sour cream
4 tablespoons mayonnaise
2 tablespoons white vinegar
½ teaspoon celery seed
½ teaspoon dry mustard
½ teaspoon black pepper
2 teaspoons salt

Recipe doubles easily for a crowd. Perfect for a barbecue.

Place vegetables in a large bowl. Combine remaining ingredients and pour over vegetables. Cover and refrigerate overnight.

Yield: 10 to 12 servings.

Artichoke Salad

1 (8-ounce) package chicken-flavored vermicelli-rice mix
1 (6¼-ounce) package fried rice mix with almonds
½ cup chopped green bell pepper
½ cup chopped onion
½ cup pimento-stuffed olives
2 (6-ounce) jars marinated artichoke hearts, drained and thinly sliced
1 teaspoon curry powder
½ cup mayonnaise

Prepare rice mixes according to package directions. Cool and add remaining ingredients. Mix well, cover and chill.

Marinated Vegetable Salad

1 clove garlic
1 can artichoke hearts, drained
2 jars whole mushrooms, drained
1 can black olives, drained
1 can hearts of palm, drained
1 can baby corn, drained
2 tomatoes, quartered
3 green onions, chopped
Cauliflower florets, optional
Water chestnuts, optional
1 bottle Italian dressing

Crush garlic clove in a salad bowl. Add vegetables and top with dressing. Cover and chill until ready to serve.

Yield: 6 to 8 servings.

Broccoli Raisin Delight Salad

1 cup mayonnaise
2 tablespoons apple cider vinegar
½ cup sugar
Florets from 2 bunches of broccoli
½ cup raisins
½ cup chopped pecans
½ cup chopped purple onion
12 slices bacon, crisp-fried and crumbled

Combine mayonnaise, vinegar and sugar in a small bowl and mix well. Chill overnight. Combine broccoli, raisins, pecans and onion in a large salad bowl. Add dressing and toss thoroughly. Garnish with bacon.

Yield: 10 servings.

Crunchy Cauliflower Salad

1 large head cauliflower, broken into florets
1 cup sliced radishes
½ cup sliced green onions
1 (8-ounce) can sliced water chestnuts, drained
¾ cup sour cream
¾ cup mayonnaise
2 tablespoons caraway seeds
1 small package buttermilk salad dressing mix

Place cauliflower, radishes, green onions and water chestnuts in a medium mixing bowl and toss gently. Combine remaining ingredients and blend well. Pour over vegetables and stir to coat. Spoon into a serving bowl, cover and chill before serving.

Yield: 6 to 8 servings.

Perfect for church suppers.

Feta and Vegetable Salad

7 ounces Feta cheese, crumbled
1 cucumber, peeled and chopped
1 tomato, peeled and chopped
½ large red onion, chopped
3 tablespoons olive oil
2 tablespoons fresh lemon juice
Pepper
Chopped fresh parsley

Combine all ingredients except pepper and parsley in a large bowl. Season with pepper and toss well. Cover and chill thoroughly. Garnish with parsley before serving.

Yield: 4 servings.

Delicious with steak.

"He is happiest, be he king or peasant who finds peace in his home."
—Goethe

Warm Mushroom Salad with Pistou Vinaigrette

½ pound shiitake mushrooms, cut in 1½-inch pieces
½ pound oyster mushrooms, cut in 1½-inch pieces
¼ cup dry white wine
¼ cup olive oil, divided
¾ teaspoon salt
Freshly ground pepper
2 cloves garlic
¼ cup grated Romano cheese
1¼ cups fresh herbs - basil, parsley, thyme and oregano
6 ounces mixed greens
1 tablespoon sherry vinegar

Place mushrooms on a large piece of foil. Season with wine, 3 tablespoons of oil, salt and pepper. Slice 1 clove of garlic and place on mushrooms. Fold foil to make a loose package and bake in a preheated 350° oven for 15 to 20 minutes. Remove to a large bowl. Chop remaining garlic and add to mushrooms. Add cheese and herbs, toss, and season to taste. Place the greens in a bowl and toss with remaining oil, salt, pepper and vinegar. Arrange greens on serving plates and top with mushroom mixture. Garnish with shavings of Romano cheese.

Creamy Potato Salad

3 pounds red potatoes
2 cups mayonnaise
1 cup sour cream
½ cup chopped celery
1 package original Ranch dressing
1 small bunch green onions, chopped
Salt and pepper to taste

This unusual potato salad is sure to be a hit on any occasion.

Boil potatoes until done. Drain and cool. Combine remaining ingredients in a salad bowl. Add potatoes and toss to coat. Cover and refrigerate overnight.

Yield: 6 servings.

"Beauty of style and harmony and grace and good rhythm depend on simplicity."
—Plato

Sunshine Salad

I	package lemon gelatin
⅔	cup boiling water
I	cup crushed pineapple, drained and juice reserved
⅔	cup evaporated milk
I½	teaspoons vinegar
I	(8-ounce) package cream cheese, softened
2	carrots, grated
½	cup golden raisins

Dissolve gelatin in water. Add reserved syrup, milk and vinegar and mix well. Blend in cream cheese until smooth. Add remaining ingredients and mix thoroughly. Pour into a 2-quart mold until set, 2 to 3 hours, or overnight.

A bright, cheery salad with a delightful tangy-sweet taste.

A Simple Pleasure...

The moment of recognition that comes when we pick up the phone and hear the voice of a dear friend we haven't spoken to for a long time.

Alaskan Fruit Salad

I	envelope unflavored gelatin
I½	cups orange juice, divided
I	(3-ounce) package regular vanilla pudding mix
I	cup frozen whipped topping, thawed
I	small can mandarin oranges, drained
I	(8-ounce) can crushed pineapple, drained
¼	cup maraschino cherries, quartered

Soften gelatin in ¼ cup orange juice. Place in a saucepan and add remaining juice and pudding mix. Cook over medium heat until mixture bubbles and thickens. Chill until partially set. Fold in remaining ingredients and turn into a 4-cup mold. Chill until firm, about 4 to 5 hours or overnight.

Yield: 6 servings.

Ambrosia Salad

4   bananas, sliced
3   large red apples, peeled and
    chopped
3   large oranges, peeled and
    chopped
2   (6-ounce) cans fruit salad,
    drained
1   (6-ounce) bag walnuts, chopped
10 ounces sour cream
1   (8-ounce) bag shredded
    coconut, divided

Combine fresh and canned fruit in a serving bowl. Stir in walnuts, sour cream and half of coconut. Cover and refrigerate for at least 1 hour. Sprinkle with remaining coconut just before serving.

Peach Congealed Salad

1   large package peach gelatin
2   cups boiling water
1   can peach pie filling
1   small can crushed pineapple,
    drained
1   (8-ounce) package cream
    cheese, softened
½   cup sugar
8   ounces sour cream
Grated cheese
Chopped pecans

Dissolve gelatin in boiling water. Add pie filling and pineapple and pour into mold to congeal. Combine cream cheese and sugar and mix until well blended. Stir in sour cream. Pour over congealed gelatin mixture and chill until set. Garnish with cheese and pecans before serving.

Cherry Cola Salad

1   can cherry pie filling
¾   cup sugar
1   cup water, divided
1   large box cherry gelatin
1   cup cola
1   small can crushed pineapple,
    drained
1   cup crushed pecans

Place pie filling, sugar and ½ cup water in a large saucepan. Bring to a boil, stirring. Put gelatin in a 2½-quart serving dish. Pour hot mixture over and stir to dissolve. Stir in cola and remaining water. Add pineapple and nuts and chill until set.

Pink Arctic Frozen Fruit Salad

1 (8-ounce) package cream cheese, softened
2 tablespoons mayonnaise
2 tablespoons sugar
1 (8-ounce) can whole cranberry sauce
1 cup crushed pineapple, drained
½ cup chopped walnuts or pecans
1 cup prepared whipped topping

Combine all ingredients except whipped topping and blend thoroughly. Fold in whipped topping. Place paper muffin cups in muffin tins and fill with mixture. Freeze. When frozen place in a plastic bag and keep in freezer until ready to use.

Yield: 8 to 10 servings.

Buttermilk Salad

1 large can crushed pineapple
1 large package strawberry gelatin
2 cups buttermilk
1 large container frozen whipped topping, thawed
Chopped nuts

Combine pineapple and gelatin in a saucepan. Bring to a boil, remove from heat and cool. Stir in buttermilk and mix well. Fold in whipped topping and nuts. Pour into a mold and chill until set.

Easy Cranberry Salad

1 (6-ounce) box strawberry gelatin
1½ cups boiling water
1 (16-ounce) can jellied cranberry sauce
1 (11-ounce) can mandarin orange slices, drained and halved
1 (16-ounce) can crushed pineapple, well-drained
¾ cup chopped pecans

Dissolve gelatin in boiling water. Mash cranberry sauce and add to gelatin mixture. Stir in remaining ingredients and pour into an oiled 2-quart mold. Refrigerate until set and serve chilled.

Yield 8 to 10 servings.

Mandarin Salad

1   small box orange gelatin
1   cup boiling water
½   (6-ounce) can frozen orange
    juice concentrate
¾   orange juice can cold water
1   tablespoon lemon juice
1   (9-ounce) can crushed
    pineapple
1   (11-ounce) can mandarin
    oranges, drained

Dissolve gelatin in boiling water. Add half of a can of orange juice concentrate (save remainder for other uses), water, lemon juice and pineapple. Let stand until mixture begins to thicken. Add oranges and chill until firm.

Strawberry Pretzel Salad

2   cups pretzels, crushed
¾   cup margarine, melted
1   cup plus 4 tablespoons sugar,
    divided
1   (8-ounce) package cream
    cheese, softened
1   (8-ounce) container frozen
    whipped topping, thawed
1   (6-ounce) package
    strawberry gelatin
2   cups boiling water
1   (16-ounce) package frozen
    sliced strawberries

Combine crushed pretzels, margarine and 4 tablespoons sugar. Press into bottom of a 9 x 13-inch baking pan and bake in a preheated 325° oven for 8 minutes. Cool completely. Combine cream cheese and remaining sugar and beat until light and fluffy. Fold whipped topping into cream cheese mixture. Spread over cooled crust, cover and refrigerate. Dissolve gelatin in boiling water and add strawberries. Refrigerate until thickened. Pour over cream cheese mixture and refrigerate until set.

Yield: 15 to 20 servings.

"That man is the richest whose pleasures are the cheapest."
   —Thoreau

Frozen Strawberry Salad

1　(8-ounce) package cream cheese, softened
½　cup sugar
1　large package frozen sliced strawberries
1　large can crushed pineapple, drained
½　cup chopped pecans
1　(8-ounce) container frozen whipped topping, thawed

Combine cream cheese and sugar and mix until light and fluffy. Stir in strawberries, pineapple and nuts. Fold in whipped topping and turn into a 9 x 13-inch pan or muffin cups. Freeze. If using pan, cut into squares to serve. Serve as a salad or dessert.

Mandarin Orange Salad

DRESSING:

¼　cup vegetable oil
2　tablespoons white vinegar
2　tablespoons sugar
1　tablespoon snipped parsley
½　teaspoon salt
Dash of pepper
Dash of hot pepper sauce

For Dressing: Combine all ingredients in a tightly covered jar, shake to blend and refrigerate at least 1 hour.

SALAD:

¼　cup slivered almonds
1　tablespoon plus 1 teaspoon sugar
½　head Romaine lettuce
½　head Bibb lettuce
1　cup chopped celery
3　green onions, thinly sliced
1　(11-ounce) can mandarin oranges, drained

For Salad: cook and stir almonds and sugar in a skillet over low heat until sugar is melted and nuts are coated. Turn onto waxed paper, cool, break apart and set aside. Place lettuces, celery and onions in a plastic bag. Fasten bag securely and refrigerate. Pour dressing into bag 5 minutes before serving. Add oranges and shake until well coated. Add almonds and shake again. Pour into serving bowl, toss and serve.

Yield: 4 servings.

Oriental Slaw

1   head of cabbage, finely
    shredded
¼   cup sliced almonds
¼   cup sunflower kernels
1   bunch green onions,
    chopped
1   package ramen noodle soup
    mix, chicken or oriental
    flavor

Place cabbage, almonds, sunflower kernels and green onions in a serving bowl. Crumble dry noodles over top. Combine all dressing ingredients and pour over cabbage mixture. Toss to coat.

DRESSING:

Seasoning packet from soup mix
¼   cup olive oil
3   tablespoons vinegar
2   tablespoons sugar
½   teaspoon salt
½   teaspoon pepper

Sweet Colorful Cole Slaw

1   cup sugar
½   cup water
½   cup white vinegar
1   teaspoon mustard seed
2   tablespoons salt or more to
    taste
2   cups cold water
1   quart shredded cabbage
1   onion, chopped
½   cup chopped pimento
½   cup chopped green bell
    pepper
3   cups diced celery
2   carrots, grated

Combine sugar, ½ cup water, vinegar and mustard seed in a saucepan. Bring to a boil, stirring, until sugar is dissolved. Remove from heat and cool. Dissolve salt in cold water to make a brine. Add cabbage, onion, pimento and bell pepper. Soak for 30 minutes. Drain well and squeeze out any excess moisture. Add celery and carrots and place in a large serving bowl. Pour syrup over mixture and toss to coat. Cover and chill overnight.

Yield: 8 servings.

This cool and crisp slaw stays fresh for several days.

Crispy Bacon Cole Slaw

¾ cup salad dressing
1 tablespoon sugar
4 cups shredded cabbage
1 cup shredded red cabbage
¼ cup shredded carrot, optional
½ cup chopped peanuts
4 slices bacon, crisply cooked and crumbled

Combine salad dressing and sugar in a large bowl. Add remaining ingredients and mix lightly. Cover and refrigerate until chilled.

Yield: 10 servings.

Note: Light dressing may be used.

Crowd-Pleasing Cole Slaw

1 head cabbage, grated or 1 bag shredded cabbage
1 medium green bell pepper, chopped
1 bunch green onions, chopped
1 medium tomato, chopped
2 tablespoons mayonnaise
1½ teaspoon salt

Combine all ingredients and serve.

Yield: 8 to 10 servings.

Poppy Seed Chicken Salad

3 (5-ounce) cans premium white chicken, drained
1 red apple, diced
1 cup red or green grapes, chopped
1 bunch green onions, chopped
½ cup walnuts
3 tablespoons poppy seed dressing

Combine all ingredients except dressing. Drizzle with dressing and serve in pastry shells as an appetizer, in croissants or over lettuce as a salad.

Yield: 12 servings.

Almond Chicken Salad

1 (4-pound) chicken
2 cups finely chopped celery
½ cup slivered almonds
1 egg, well beaten
½ teaspoon salt
1 tablespoon dry mustard
⅜ cup sugar, or to taste
⅜ cup cider vinegar
1 heaping tablespoon flour
Pinch of cayenne pepper
Mayonnaise

Place chicken in a large pot and cover with water. Add salt and bring to a boil. Reduce heat and simmer slowly until chicken falls from bone. Remove from broth. Reserve ½ cup broth for dressing. When chicken is cool enough to handle, skin and debone. Cut into bite-size pieces and place in a serving bowl. Add celery and almonds. Place remaining ingredients, including reserved broth, in top of a double boiler and cook, stirring, over slowly boiling water until thickened. Measure the amount of this mixture and add an equal amount of mayonnaise. Pour over chicken mixture and stir until blended.

"Go confidently in the direction of your dreams! Live the life you've imagined. As you simplify your life, the laws of the universe will be simpler."

—Henry David Thoreau

Curry Artichoke Rice Salad

2 cups chicken broth
1 cup rice
¼ cup diced green onion
¼ cup pimentos
2 (6-ounce) jars artichoke hearts, drained
½ cup mayonnaise
½ teaspoon curry powder
1 teaspoon dill
1 (8-ounce) can water chestnuts, drained

Bring chicken broth to a boil in a medium saucepan. Stir in rice and simmer, covered, until rice is cooked. Cool slightly and place in a large serving bowl. Add remaining ingredients, cover and chill.

Yield: 8 servings.
Covington's

Wild Rice and Chicken Salad

3 (8-ounce) boxes long-grain and wild rice mix
5 cups cooked, chopped chicken (about 1¾ pounds)
½ pound seedless green grapes, halved
½ pound seedless red grapes, halved
1 (7-ounce) bag sliced almonds, toasted

DRESSING:

1 cup mayonnaise
⅓ cup honey
3 tablespoons lemon juice
3 tablespoons tarragon cider vinegar
⅓ cup chopped green onions
3 tablespoons chopped fresh parsley
1 teaspoon pepper
½ teaspoon salt

Cook rice according to package directions and place in a large salad bowl. Add chicken. Combine all dressing ingredients and pour over rice mixture. Cover and chill at least 6 hours. Add remaining ingredients just before serving. Toss and serve.

Yield: 18 servings.

Macaroni Salad

1 small package macaroni, cooked according to package directions and drained
1 medium cucumber, chopped
1 bunch green onions, chopped
1 medium tomato, chopped
2 tablespoons mayonnaise
1½ teaspoons seasoning salt

Combine all ingredients and serve.

Yield: 8 to 10 servings.

Ramen Noodle Salad

DRESSING:

½ cup canola oil
2 tablespoons light soy sauce
¼ cup sugar
¼ cup apple cider vinegar

For Dressing: Combine all ingredients, cover, and chill overnight.

SALAD:

1 head Romaine lettuce
Florets from 1 head broccoli
4 green onions, finely chopped
2 packages ramen noodle soup mix (seasoning omitted)
½ cup butter, melted
⅓ cup sunflower seeds
½ cup slivered almonds

For Salad: Toss together lettuce, broccoli and green onions. Break up noodles and sauté in butter with sunflower seeds and almonds. Add to lettuce mixture just before serving. Top with dressing and toss until thoroughly blended.

Wonderful with beef, pork or chicken.

"When we lack proper time for the simple pleasures of life, for the enjoyment of eating, drinking, playing, creating, visiting friends, and watching children at play, then we have missed the purpose of life. Not on bread alone do we live, but on all these human and heart-hungry luxuries."

—Ed Hayes

Breakfast, Brunch and Breads

Thimble Biscuits

For Annie Wade Hays

Proud Annie Wade Hays, celebrating her 90s these days,
Indeed is a marvel to behold with her kitchen sashays.
A champ she is at turning chores to fun
and entertaining kiddies on the run.
In long past days as children came along,
she was most clever in teaching her little throng.
Their gleeful shouts rang out when she would say,
"Today we're making thimble biscuits as we play."
She mixed and stirred and rolled the ready dough,
and each child pressed a thimble biscuit just so-so.
Then into oven they'd rise in golden bake
to eat with jam and butter that's better than cake!
And all because their mom's sharp mind was nimble
to let the kids carve biscuits with a thimble!

Ralph Hammond
Poet Laureate Emeritus, State of Alabama

Note: Mr. Hammond is the husband of former member, Myra Hammond. He wrote this poem as a tribute to Annie Wade Hays. She is the mother of John Hays, developer of Haysland Square in Huntsville.

French Breakfast Puffs

⅓ cup shortening or butter
1 cup sugar, divided
1 egg
1½ cups flour, sifted
1½ teaspoons baking powder
½ teaspoon salt
¼ teaspoon nutmeg
½ cup milk
⅓ cup butter, melted
1 teaspoon cinnamon

Beat shortening and ½ cup sugar until light and fluffy. Add egg and mix well. Sift together flour, baking powder, salt and nutmeg. Add to creamed mixture alternately with milk. Fill greased muffin cups two-thirds full. Bake in preheated 350° oven until golden brown, about 20 minutes. Remove from oven and roll immediately in melted butter, then in mixture of cinnamon and remaining sugar. Serve hot.

Yield: 3 dozen miniature or 2 dozen medium muffins.

Sunday Morning Flapjacks

4   eggs, separated
2   cups sifted all-purpose flour
2   teaspoons baking powder
½   teaspoon salt
2   tablespoons sugar
6   tablespoons melted butter or
     margarine
2   cups milk

Place all ingredients except egg whites in a large mixing bowl and beat with mixer until well blended. In a separate bowl, beat egg whites until stiff but not dry and fold into batter. Using 1 tablespoon batter for each pancake, cook on a hot griddle until surface is dry. Turn and continue cooking until done.

Yield: 4 to 5 servings.

Variation: To serve as dessert, top with shaved maple sugar or fruit sauce and whipped cream.

Personalized Pancakes
PANCAKE BATTER

A thrill for a child to have a stack of pancakes with his name on top!

Dip a teaspoon into batter and let excess drip off. Using batter left on tip of spoon, draw letters BACK-WARDS on a hot, greased griddle. When underside is lightly browned, pour another spoonful of batter over letters to completely surround them. Bake until bubbles appear, then turn and brown second side. The letters will stand out from the surrounding pancake.

MAPLE SYRUP

2   cups sugar
1   cup water
½   teaspoon maple flavoring

Mix sugar and water in a saucepan. Bring to a boil, stirring. Turn off, leaving syrup on burner to cool. Add flavoring. May be made in microwave.

German Apple Pancake

3 large eggs
⅔ cup half and half
½ cup all-purpose flour
4 tablespoons melted unsalted butter, divided
4 tablespoons sugar, divided
¾ teaspoon cinnamon, divided
Pinch of salt
1 large green apple, peeled, cored, and sliced
1 teaspoon powdered sugar

Mix eggs, cream, flour, 2 tablespoons butter, 1 tablespoon sugar, ½ teaspoon cinnamon and salt in a bowl. Set aside. (Can be made a day ahead and refrigerated. Stir before using.) Preheat oven to 450°. Brush remaining butter on bottom and sides of a 10-inch cast-iron skillet. Place apple slices over butter. Sprinkle with remaining sugar and cinnamon. Cook over medium heat until apple is just tender, about 6 minutes, stirring occasionally. Pour batter over apples and place skillet in oven. Bake until pancake is puffed and deep brown, about 15 minutes. Remove from oven, cut around edges of pancake and invert onto a serving dish. Sift powdered sugar over top and serve with heated syrup, if desired.

Yield: 2 servings.

Grandmother's Waffles

½ cup shortening
3 tablespoons sugar
3 eggs, separated
2 cups flour
½ teaspoon salt
3 teaspoons baking powder
1 cup milk

Cream shortening and sugar. Add egg yolks and beat well. Combine flour, salt and baking powder and add to shortening mixture alternately with milk, beating some after each addition. Beat egg whites in a separate bowl until stiff but not dry. Fold into batter. Pour in prepared waffle iron and cook until golden brown.

Variation: Pecans or chocolate chips may be added while cooking.

Yield: 4 to 6 servings.

Everyday French Toast

4   egg whites, lightly beaten
½   cup skim milk
2   tablespoons frozen orange
    juice concentrate
1   teaspoon vanilla
½   teaspoon cinnamon
4   slices whole wheat bread
2   tablespoons all-fruit jam

Beat together egg whites, milk, orange juice concentrate, vanilla and cinnamon. Add bread slices one at a time, allowing bread to absorb liquid. Coat a skillet with nonstick spray and heat. Gently lift each bread slice with a spatula and place in skillet. Cook until golden brown on both sides. Serve topped with ½ tablespoon of jam per slice.

Leftovers may be frozen in individual freezer bags and toasted to reheat.

Yield: 4 servings.

Blueberry Muffins

Juice of 1 lemon
½   cup milk
2   cups biscuit mix
½   cup sugar
2   tablespoons margarine,
    softened
1   egg
1   cup blueberries

TOPPING:

4   tablespoons sugar
4   tablespoons margarine,
    melted

Line muffin tins with paper muffin cups. Pour lemon juice into a cup measure and add enough milk to make ⅔ cup liquid. Combine biscuit mix, sugar, margarine and milk mixture. Fold in blueberries and spoon into muffin cups. Bake in preheated 400° oven for 25 minutes. Remove from pan and dip top of each muffin in melted margarine and then sugar.

For special brunches, use oversize muffin tins to make 6 Texas-size muffins.

Yield: 1 dozen.

"In the end, what affects your life most deeply are things too simple to talk about."

—Nell Blaine

Cheese Muffins

2   tablespoons butter or
    margarine, divided
½   cup chopped onion
1½ cups biscuit mix
1   cup shredded sharp cheese,
    divided
1   large egg, lightly beaten
½   cup milk
1   tablespoon sesame seeds,
    toasted

Melt 1 tablespoon butter in a skillet over medium heat. Add onion and sauté, stirring constantly, until tender, about 3 minutes. Place onion, biscuit mix and ½ cup cheese in a large bowl. Combine egg and milk and add to onion mixture, stirring just until moistened. Spoon into greased muffin pans, filling half-full. Sprinkle with remaining cheese and sesame seeds and dot with remaining butter. Bake in preheated 400° oven until done, about 13 minutes.

Yield: 1 dozen.

"For where your treasure is, there will your heart be also."
—Matthew 6:21

Easy Yeast Muffins

1   egg, lightly beaten
½   cup sugar
¾   cup vegetable oil
4½ cups self-rising flour
1   package dry yeast
2   cups warm-to-hot water

Combine egg, sugar and oil. Add flour and mix. In a separate bowl, mix yeast and water. Add to flour mixture and stir with a spoon. Coat muffin pans with nonstick spray and fill three-quarters full with dough. Bake in preheated 400° oven until brown, about 15 minutes. Dough will keep, covered, in refrigerator for up to one week.

Variation: For Cheese Muffins, add 1 cup shredded cheese to dough.

Yield: 1½ to 2 dozen muffins.

Kudzu Jelly

4   cups kudzu blooms
4   cups boiling water
1   tablespoon lemon juice
1   (1¾-ounce) package pectin
5   cups sugar

Wash blooms with cold water and place in a large bowl. Pour boiling water over blooms, cover and chill at least 8 hours. Pour liquid through a colander into a Dutch oven and discard blooms. (Liquid will be gray until lemon juice is added.) Add lemon juice and pectin to liquid. Bring to a full boil over high heat, stirring constantly. Stir in sugar and return to a full boil for 1 minute. Remove from heat and skim off foam with a metal spoon. Quickly pour jelly into hot sterilized jars, filling to ¼ inch from top. Wipe rim and cover at once with metal lids and screw on bands.

Yield: 6 half-pints.

Note: A pretty pink jelly that's a great conversation piece.

Cranberry Apple Pear Casserole

1½ cups frozen cranberries
3   Granny Smith apples, sliced
3   pears, sliced, or 2 cans pears, drained and sliced

Layer apples, cranberries and pears in a greased 9 x 13-inch baking dish.

TOPPING:

¾   cup butter or margarine
1½ cups firmly packed brown sugar
1½ cups oats
¾   cup pecans

Especially good with chicken.

For Topping: Melt butter in a medium saucepan. Stir in brown sugar until well blended. Add oats and pecans and mix well. Pour over fruit and bake in a preheated 350° oven 45 minutes to 1 hour.

Covington's

Yield: 8 to 10 servings.

Hot Curried Fruit

1 (29-ounce) can fruit for salad, drained
1 (16-ounce) can pineapple tidbits, drained
½ cup red cherries, drained
½ cup melted margarine
1 cup firmly packed brown sugar
2 tablespoons cornstarch
1 teaspoon curry powder, optional
Bananas, quartered

Combine all fruit except bananas and top with margarine. Mix brown sugar, cornstarch and curry powder, if desired, and sprinkle over fruit. Stir to coat. Place in a 9 x 13-inch casserole and bake in a preheated 350° oven for 40 minutes. Add bananas and stir. Serve warm.

Yield: 8 to 10 servings.

Gala Fresh Fruit Bowl

6 medium oranges
¼ cup sifted confectioners sugar
1 pint fresh or frozen strawberries, halved
2 kiwi fruit, peeled and sliced ¼-inch thick
⅓ cup shredded coconut

Peel and section oranges over a large glass serving bowl to catch juices. Place segments in bowl and sprinkle with sugar. Toss to coat. Gently stir in strawberries and kiwi. Cover and chill until serving time. Just before serving, sprinkle with coconut.

Yield: 8 servings.

Baked Fruit

⅓ cup butter, melted
1 (16-ounce) jar applesauce
Peaches, sliced
Pears, sliced
Pineapple chunks
Cherries
3 bananas, quartered
½ cup chopped nuts
Brown sugar

Combine butter and applesauce in a baking dish. Add fruit and nuts and stir to mix. Sprinkle with brown sugar and bake in a preheated 350° oven for 30 minutes.

Cheese Grits

1   cup quick grits
1   teaspoon salt
4   cups water
1   roll garlic cheese, cut up
½   cup butter
½   cup milk
2   eggs, beaten
Grated Cheddar cheese

Cook grits slowly in salted water until done. Stir in garlic cheese and butter. Add milk and eggs and blend well. Pour into a greased casserole dish and bake in a preheated 350° oven for 40 minutes. Remove from oven and sprinkle with grated cheese. Bake an additional 5 minutes.

A great way to introduce non-Southerners to grits.

Sausage Balls in Apple Butter

1   pound mild bulk pork
    sausage
1   large jar apple butter

Roll sausage into marble-sized balls. Sauté in skillet until done and drain on paper towels. Heat apple butter in a saucepan or chafing dish and add sausage balls. Keep warm while serving.

Yield: 5 dozen.

Sausage Breakfast Casserole

6   slices bread
Butter or margarine
1   pound bulk pork sausage
1½ cups (6 ounces) shredded
    longhorn cheese
6   eggs, beaten
2   cups half and half
1   teaspoon salt

Remove crusts from bread and spread with butter. Place in a greased 9 x 13-inch baking dish. Cook sausage until browned, stirring to crumble. Drain well and spoon over bread. Sprinkle with cheese. Combine remaining ingredients and mix well. Pour over cheese and cover. Refrigerate overnight. Remove from refrigerator 15 minutes before baking. Bake, uncovered, in a preheated 350° oven until set, about 45 minutes.

Yield: 8 servings.

Christy's Breakfast Quiche

1	tablespoon margarine
1	medium red bell pepper, chopped
1	medium onion, chopped
4	ounces fresh mushrooms, sliced
1	pound sausage
5	eggs, lightly beaten
1	cup shredded Monterey Jack cheese
1	package frozen chopped broccoli
1	cup ricotta cheese
1	tablespoon parsley flakes
20	frozen filo dough sheets
1	cup butter, melted

Melt margarine in a large skillet over medium heat. Add bell pepper, onion and mushroom and sauté until tender. Remove from skillet. Brown sausage, crumble and drain. Add to mushroom mixture. Combine broccoli, ricotta cheese and parsley in another bowl. Heat oven to 350°. Unroll filo sheets and cover with a towel. Place 1 sheet in an ungreased 9 x 13-inch pan and fold it to fit. Brush with melted butter. Repeat with 4 more sheets and butter. Spread half of mushroom mixture over top. Layer 5 more filo sheets and butter over mushrooms. Spread with all of broccoli mixture. Repeat layering with 5 more filo sheets and butter. Spread remaining mushroom mixture over top. Finish with remaining filo and butter. Bake until brown, 50 to 60 minutes.

Yield: 10 servings.

German Banana Nut Bread

2	cups sugar
½	cup butter, softened
½	cup shortening
¾	cup milk
1	(8-ounce) container sour cream
2	eggs
4	not-too-ripe bananas, mashed
3	cups self-rising flour
1	teaspoon vanilla
1	cup chopped walnuts

Cream sugar, butter and shortening. Add remaining ingredients and beat for 3 minutes. Turn into 2 greased and floured loaf pans and bake in a preheated 350° oven until a tester inserted in center comes out clean, about 1 hour.

Bacon and Double Cheese Quiche

CRUST:

1⅓ cups all-purpose flour
⅛ teaspoon salt
½ cup chilled butter, cut into small pieces
2-3 tablespoons cold water

FILLING:

4 large eggs, lightly beaten
1½ cups half and half
¼ teaspoon dried thyme
⅛ teaspoon white pepper
10 strips lean bacon, cooked crisp and crumbled
½ cup shredded Gruyère cheese
½ cup shredded white Cheddar cheese

For Crust: Mix together flour and salt. Cut in butter with a pastry blender until coarse crumbs form. Add water 1 tablespoon at a time, tossing with a fork, until a dough forms. Shape into a disk, wrap in plastic wrap and refrigerate for 30 minutes. Preheat oven to 375°. Roll dough into an 11-inch circle on a lightly floured surface. Fit into a 9-inch pie pan and trim edges, leaving a ¼-inch overhang. Fold under to form a stand-up edge. Prick dough with a fork and bake until lightly golden, about 10 minutes. Transfer to a wire rack to cool.

For Filling: Whisk together eggs, cream, thyme and pepper. Pour into prepared crust and sprinkle with bacon pieces and both cheeses. Bake until golden and custard is set, about 30 minutes. Serve warm.

Yield: 8 servings.

Mama's Best Banana Bread

½ cup shortening
1 cup sugar
1 egg
1 teaspoon baking soda dissolved in ½ cup hot water
1 teaspoon baking powder
Pinch of salt
2 cups flour
2 large bananas, mashed
1 cup chopped pecans, optional

Cream shortening and sugar. Add remaining ingredients and beat until well blended. Pour into a greased loaf pan and bake in a preheated 350° oven until a tester inserted in center comes out clean, 1 to 1 hour and 15 minutes.

Upper Crust Chicken

10 slices white bread
2 cups chopped, cooked chicken
1 cup chopped celery
2 cups shredded sharp cheese, divided
1 cup mayonnaise
2 eggs, lightly beaten
½ teaspoon poultry seasoning
1½ cups milk

A great prepare-ahead-recipe.

Trim crusts from bread, reserving crusts. Cut bread diagonally into quarters. Cube reserved crusts and combine with chicken, celery and 1¾ cups cheese. Mix well and spoon into an 8 x 12-inch baking dish. Arrange bread quarters in an overlapping pattern over chicken. Combine mayonnaise, eggs, and seasoning in a large bowl and blend well. Gradually add milk, mixing until blended. Pour over bread and sprinkle with remaining cheese. Cover and refrigerate several hours or overnight. Bake, uncovered, in a preheated 375° oven until set, about 30 minutes. Garnish with celery leaves, if desired.

Yield: 8 servings.

Cream Cheese Danish

2 large cans refrigerated crescent rolls
2 (8-ounce) packages cream cheese, softened
¾ cup sugar
1 egg, separated
1 teaspoon vanilla
1 teaspoon lemon juice

GLAZE:

1 tablespoon margarine, melted
1 cup confectioners sugar
Milk

Unroll 1 package of rolls and spread in a greased 9 x 13-inch baking pan. Combine cream cheese, sugar, egg yolk, vanilla and lemon juice. Spread over rolls. Unroll remaining rolls and place over cream cheese mixture. Brush with egg white and bake in a preheated 350° oven for 25 minutes.

For Glaze: Mix margarine and confectioners sugar. Add enough milk to reach desired consistency. Spread on warm pastry and cut into squares.

Pecan Cranberry Biscotti

1½ cups pecan halves, toasted and divided
1 teaspoon baking powder
2½ cups all-purpose flour
1¼ cups sugar
⅛ teaspoon salt
4 large eggs
1 teaspoon vanilla
1 cup dried cranberries
Grated peel of 1 lemon

Preheat oven to 350°. Finely chop ¾ cup pecans and set aside. Combine baking powder, flour, sugar and salt in a mixing bowl. Beat eggs and vanilla together in another bowl. Add to dry ingredients and beat on medium-low speed until a stiff dough forms. Stir in chopped pecans, cranberries and zest. Turn dough onto a well-floured board and sprinkle with additional flour. Knead slightly and shape into 9 x 3½-inch logs. Transfer to a greased jelly roll sheet and bake until golden brown, about 25 to 30 minutes. Remove from oven until cool enough to handle, about 10 minutes. Reduce oven temperature to 275°. On cutting board, slice logs on diagonal into ¾-inch thick pieces. Return pieces, cut-side down, to baking sheet. Bake until lightly toasted, about 20 minutes. Turn over and continue baking until slightly dry, about 20 more minutes. Cool on a wire rack. Store in an air-tight container.

Yield: 2 dozen.

Zucchini Bread

3 eggs, lightly beaten
2½ cups sugar
1 cup vegetable oil
3 cups self-rising flour
3 teaspoons cinnamon
1 tablespoon coconut flavoring
1 tablespoon vanilla
2 cups grated zucchini
1 cup chopped nuts

Combine all ingredients and pour into 3 well-greased and floured loaf pans or 1 large tube pan. Bake in a preheated 350° oven until a tester inserted in center comes out clean, 45 to 50 minutes.

Yield: 3 loaves.

Cranberry Sour Cream Crumble

¼ cup chopped almonds
2 cups flour
1¼ teaspoons baking powder
½ teaspoon baking soda
¼ teaspoon salt
1 cup sugar
½ cup butter, softened
1 teaspoon vanilla
2 eggs
1 cup light or nonfat sour cream
1 cup whole cranberry sauce

TOPPING:

¼ cup chopped almonds
½ cup flour
⅓ cup sugar
¼ cup melted butter
½ teaspoon vanilla

Sprinkle ¼ cup almonds in a greased springform or 10-inch tube pan and set aside. Combine flour, baking powder, baking soda and salt in a large bowl and mix well. Cream sugar, butter and vanilla in a mixing bowl at medium speed 1 to 2 minutes, scraping bowl frequently. Add eggs and beat until well mixed, scraping bowl frequently. Add flour mixture and sour cream alternately, beating until well mixed. Spread half of batter in prepared pan. Cover with cranberry sauce. Top with remaining batter. Combine all topping ingredients and sprinkle over batter. Bake in a preheated 350° oven until a tester inserted near center comes out clean, about 1 hour and 15 minutes. Cool in pan on a wire rack for 10 minutes.

Yield: 12 servings.

Orange Blossoms

3 eggs
1⅓ cups sugar
¼ cup water
1½ cups all-purpose flour
1½ teaspoons baking powder
½ teaspoon salt
1 teaspoon vanilla

ICING:

1 (1-pound) box confectioners sugar
1¼ cups orange juice
Grated peel of 2 large oranges
¼ cup lemon juice
Grated peel of 1 lemon

Perfect for a bridal tea.

Beat eggs in mixer until well-blended. Add sugar gradually and beat until well blended. Combine flour, baking powder and salt and add to egg mixture alternately with water. Spoon batter into well-greased miniature muffin tins, using 1 teaspoon for each muffin. Bake in a preheated 375° oven until done, about 10 minutes. While still warm, dip in icing and drain on wax paper.

For Icing: Mix all ingredients by hand until sugar is blended.

Yield: 100 muffins.

Lemon Tea Bread

½ cup shortening
1 cup sugar
2 eggs, lightly beaten
1⅔ cups flour
½ teaspoon salt
1 teaspoon baking powder
½ cup milk
½ cup chopped nuts
Grated peel of 1 lemon

GLAZE:

¼ cup sugar
Juice of 1 lemon

Cream shortening and sugar until fluffy. Add eggs and blend well. Mix flour, salt and baking powder and add to egg mixture alternately with milk. Beat until well-blended. Add lemon peel and nuts and pour into a greased loaf pan. Bake in a pre-heated 350° oven until a tester inserted in center comes out clean, about 1 hour. Remove from oven.

For Glaze: Dissolve sugar in lemon juice and spread over warm bread. Remove from pan to finish cooling.

Monkey Bread

4 (10-count) cans biscuits
¾ cup sugar
1 tablespoon cinnamon

GLAZE:

¾ cup sugar
½ cup firmly packed brown sugar
1¼ tablespoons cinnamon
¾ cup margarine

Cut biscuits in quarters and place in a zip-lock plastic bag. Add sugar and cinnamon and shake well. Place in a well-greased Bundt pan.

For Glaze: Place all ingredients in a saucepan and bring to a boil. Pour over biscuits and bake in a preheated 350° over for 45 minutes. Invert pan over serving dish and remove pan immediately.

Broccoli Corn Bread

1 small box corn bread mix
4 eggs, lightly beaten
1 cup grated Cheddar cheese
¼ cup chopped onion
1 (10-ounce) package frozen broccoli, thawed and squeezed dry
½ cup margarine, melted
¼ teaspoon salt

Combine all ingredients and pour into an iron skillet which has been coated with nonstick spray. Bake in a preheated 300° oven until golden brown, 30 to 40 minutes.

Even good cold.

Poppy Seed Bread

3 cups flour
1½ teaspoons salt
1½ tablespoons baking powder
1½ tablespoons poppy seeds
1½ cups vegetable oil
2⅓ cups sugar
3 eggs
1½ cups milk
1½ teaspoons vanilla
1½ teaspoons almond extract
1½ teaspoons butter flavoring

GLAZE:

½ teaspoon vanilla
½ teaspoon almond extract
½ teaspoon butter flavoring
¼ cup orange juice
¾ cup sugar

Combine flour, salt, baking powder and poppy seeds. Beat oil and sugar in a mixer until well-blended. Add eggs and beat well. Add flour mixture alternately with milk. Add flavorings and pour into 2 greased loaf pans. Bake in a preheated 325° oven until a tester inserted in center comes out clean, about 1 hour.

For Glaze: Combine all ingredients in a small saucepan and heat, stirring, until sugar is dissolved. Pour over warm bread. Cool in pans 1 hour.

Yield: 2 loaves.

Bubble Bread

1 cup milk
1½ cups sugar, divided
1 teaspoon salt
½ cup vegetable oil
1 package yeast
2 eggs, lightly beaten
4½ cups all-purpose flour
½ cup butter
1 teaspoon cinnamon
½ cup chopped nuts

Scald milk and add ½ cup sugar, salt and oil. Let cool to lukewarm and add yeast, eggs and flour. Mix until a soft dough forms. Turn onto a well-floured board and knead until dough can be handled, adding no more than 2 handfuls of additional flour. Place in a greased bowl and let rise 1 hour. Punch down and let rest 10 minutes. Melt butter. Combine remaining sugar, cinnamon and nuts in a small bowl. Pinch dough into small pieces and roll in butter, then sugar mixture. Arrange in 2 rows in a greased tube pan, making 2 layers. Cover and let rise again for about 1 hour. Bake in a preheated 350° oven for 45 minutes.

Braided Bread

1   cup milk
¼   cup butter
⅓   cup sugar
2   teaspoons salt
2   packages active dry yeast
¼   cup warm water
3   eggs
6-7 cups bread flour
Melted butter
Sesame seeds or poppy seeds
Egg white
Water

Scald milk and pour over butter, sugar and salt. Sprinkle yeast into warm water and let stand a few minutes. Stir to dissolve and add to milk mixture. Add eggs and 3 cups flour. Beat until smooth. Stir in enough flour to make a stiff dough. Turn onto a lightly floured board and knead well. Put into a greased bowl, cover and let rise until double, about 2 hours. Punch down and turn out onto board. Divide dough in half and cut each half in 3 pieces. Roll into logs about 18 inches long. Braid to form 2 loaves and brush with butter. Sprinkle with seeds, cover and let rise until doubled in size, about 45 minutes. Combine egg white and water to make an egg wash. Brush each loaf twice. Bake in a preheated 375° oven 30 to 35 minutes. Do not open oven door the first 15 minutes of baking.

Yield: 2 loaves.

Baked French Bread

1   large loaf French bread
1½ cups mayonnaise
1   cup shredded sharp Cheddar cheese
1   cup chopped green onions
3   cloves garlic, finely chopped

Cut bread in half lengthwise. Combine remaining ingredients and spread on each half. Wrap each half in aluminum foil and refrigerate 2 hours. Unwrap and bake in a preheated 350° oven 8 to 10 minutes.

Note: May be frozen before baking.

Goes well with baked spaghetti casserole.

Bread Sticks

½   cup butter, melted
2   cups self-rising flour
⅔   cup plus 2 tablespoons milk
2   tablespoons sugar

Melt butter in a 9 x 13-inch baking dish. Combine remaining ingredients and roll out on a flour surface ½ to 1-inch thick. Cut into strips and transfer to butter pan. Turn to coat. Bake in a preheated 425° oven until golden brown.

Variation: Sprinkle with poppy seeds or garlic before baking.

Sour Cream Corn Bread

¾   cup vegetable oil
1½ cups corn meal
3   eggs, lightly beaten
1   (8-ounce) container sour cream
1   medium onion, chopped
1   small can creamed corn

Combine all ingredients and pour into a greased and floured large iron skillet. Bake in a preheated 400° oven until brown.

Hushpuppies

1   egg
2   cups milk
2   tablespoons sugar
1   large onion, chopped
1   medium green bell pepper, chopped
2   tablespoons self-rising flour or biscuit mix
2-3 cups self-rising cornmeal

Beat egg, milk and sugar in a large bowl. Add remaining ingredients in order given. Stir until very stiff and drop by spoonfuls into deep, hot fat. Fry just until golden brown and floating. Drain and serve.

Yield: 4 dozen.

Chocolate Gravy

2   cups milk
1   cup water
4   tablespoons cocoa
4   tablespoons flour
¾   cup sugar
¼   teaspoon salt

Combine all ingredients in a saucepan and heat slowly, stirring, until smooth. If too thick, add more water. Serve over homemade biscuits.

Deep Freeze Yeast Rolls

3 packages yeast
1 cup warm water (115°)
1 cup shortening
1 cup boiling water
1 cup sugar
1 tablespoon salt
7 cups sifted all-purpose flour
2 eggs
Melted butter

Dissolve yeast in warm water. Place shortening in a large bowl and add boiling water. Stir until shortening melts. Cool. Add sugar, salt, yeast mixture, eggs and enough flour to make a medium-stiff dough. Turn into a large container, cover and refrigerate until doubled in size, 5 to 12 hours. Remove from refrigerator and add enough flour to make a workable dough. Roll out and cut with a small biscuit cutter. Brush with butter and fold in half. Place 2 in each muffin tin, side by side. Cover with foil and freeze. When ready to bake, put in a warm place 3 to 5 hours before baking. Bake in a preheated 350° oven until done, about 20 minutes.

Rich Rolls

1 cup scalded milk
1/3 cup butter
1/2 cup sugar
3 packages yeast
1 teaspoon sugar
1/4 cup lukewarm water
2 eggs, beaten
About 5 cups all-purpose flour
Melted butter

Combine milk, butter, sugar and salt. Cool. Soften yeast in lukewarm water with 1 teaspoon sugar. Stir and add to milk mixture. Add eggs, and about half of flour. Beat well and add enough additional flour to make a soft dough. Turn onto a floured board and knead until smooth, about 10 minutes. Place in a greased bowl and brush with melted butter. Cover and let rise until doubled in size, about 2 hours. Turn onto a floured board and form into desired shape. Brush with melted butter, place in a greased pan, cover and let rise until doubled, 1/2 to 3/4 hour. Bake in a preheated 350° oven for about 20 minutes.

Refrigerator Rolls

2   packages yeast
2   cups very warm water
½   cup sugar
1   teaspoon salt
1   egg, lightly beaten
½   cup shortening
6-7 cups all-purpose flour

Dissolve yeast in warm water. Add sugar and salt and half of flour. Add egg and shortening and blend. Add remaining flour and mix thoroughly. Turn onto floured board and knead well. Place in a bowl, cover with a hot towel and refrigerate overnight. About 2 to 3 hours before serving, turn dough onto a floured board and roll out. Shape into rolls and put in a warm place until doubled in size, 2 to 3 hours. Bake in a preheated 450° oven until done.

To Make Parkerhouse Rolls

Roll dough ½-inch thick and cut with a biscuit cutter. Brush with melted butter and make a crease across top of each roll with the back of a knife. Fold so that half of top overlaps bottom. Place rolls close together in a greased pan.

Sweet Rolls

1   package frozen homemade rolls
½   cup margarine, melted
1   package vanilla pudding mix (not instant)
⅓   cup firmly packed brown sugar
1   tablespoon cinnamon
¾   cup chopped pecans

Coat a Bundt pan with nonstick spray. Arrange rolls in pan. Pour margarine over rolls and sprinkle with remaining ingredients. Cover with plastic wrap and let sit on kitchen counter overnight. Bake in a preheated 350° oven on bottom shelf for 30 minutes.

Vegetables and

BY TY

Broccoli Casserole

2   (10-ounce) packages frozen
    broccoli
2   tablespoons grated onion
1   cup sharp Cheddar cheese
1   (10¾-ounce) can cream of
    mushroom soup
2   eggs, lightly beaten
1   cup mayonnaise
Cracker crumbs
½   cup butter, melted

Cook broccoli according to package directions and drain well. Combine onion, cheese, soup, eggs and mayonnaise. Layer half of broccoli in bottom of a greased casserole dish. Top with half of cheese mixture. Repeat layers. Sprinkle with cracker crumbs and drizzle with butter. Bake in a preheated 350° oven for 30 to 45 minutes.

Broccoli Rice Casserole

2   (10-ounce) packages frozen
    broccoli cuts or 2 bunches
    fresh broccoli
2   cups cooked rice
1   (10¾-ounce) can cream of
    mushroom soup
1   (8-ounce) jar cheese spread
3   tablespoons bread crumbs or
    cracker crumbs, buttered, if
    desired

Place broccoli in a 2-quart casserole dish and cover with plastic wrap. Cook in microwave oven on full power until tender, 10 to 11 minutes. Drain and add rice, soup and cheese spread. Pour into a 10-inch microwave-safe skillet and top with crumbs. Cook in microwave on full power until heated through, 6 to 8 minutes.

Yield: 8 servings.

 ### A Simple Pleasure...
Not wearing my watch, and more importantly not needing to.

Cabbage Casserole

1	small head cabbage, chopped
4	tablespoons butter
4	tablespoons flour
½	teaspoon salt
¼	teaspoon pepper
2	cups milk
½	pound Cheddar cheese, grated

Butter

Especially good with poultry, beef or pork.

Place chopped cabbage in a medium saucepan and cover with water. Bring to a boil, reduce heat, cover and simmer 10 minutes. Drain thoroughly. Melt butter in another saucepan. Add flour, salt and pepper and stir to blend. Gradually add milk, stirring constantly, and cook over low heat until thickened. Layer half of cabbage in a 10-inch square casserole dish. Top with half of white sauce and sprinkle with half of cheese. Repeat layers and dot with butter. Bake in a preheated 350° oven for 30 minutes.

Yield: 10 to 12 servings.

"The discovery of a new dish does more for the happiness of the human race than the discovery of a star."
—Jean Anthelme Brillat-Savarin

Corn and Green Bean Casserole

1	can French-style green beans, drained
1	can shoe peg corn, drained
1	can cream of celery soup
½	cup sour cream
½	cup grated Cheddar cheese
½	cup finely chopped onions

Salt to taste

1	sleeve round, buttery crackers, crushed
½	cup slivered almonds
¼	cup margarine, melted

Combine beans and corn and place in a greased casserole dish. Mix soup, sour cream, cheese, onions and salt and spread over vegetables. Toss cracker crumbs and almonds in melted margarine and sprinkle over top of casserole. Bake, uncovered, in a preheated 350° oven for 45 minutes.

Yield: 8 servings.

Note: May be made ahead and refrigerated overnight before baking.

Cinnamon Ring Pickles

2 gallons cucumber
2 cups lime
8½ quarts water
3 cups white vinegar, divided
1 ounce red food coloring
1 tablespoon alum
10 cups sugar
8 sticks cinnamon
1 (10-ounce) package cinnamon candy

Day 1: Peel cucumbers and slice ½-inch thick. Cut out seeds, leaving rings. Combine lime and water. Place cucumber rings in a churn and add lime mixture. Cover and let stand 24 hours.

Day 2: Drain cucumbers, rinse and cover with cold water. Soak for 3 hours and drain again. Place cucumbers in a large stock pot. Combine 1 cup vinegar, food coloring and alum. Pour over cucumbers and add enough water to cover. Bring to a boil, reduce heat and simmer 2 hours. Drain and return to churn. Combine remaining vinegar, 2 cups water, sugar, cinnamon sticks and candy in a large pot. Bring to a boil and pour over cucumbers. Let stand overnight.

Day 3: Drain liquid into a large pot, reheat and pour over pickles. Let stand 24 hours.

Day 4: Repeat Day 3.

Day 5: Heat syrup and pickles, pack into jars and seal.

Yield: 16 pints.

 A Simple Pleasure...
The aroma of something delicious wafting from the kitchen.
—Sarah Ban Breathnach

Corn Pudding

1   (16-ounce) can cream-style
    corn or 2 cups frozen cream-
    style corn
3   tablespoons flour
1   cup milk, slightly heated
3   tablespoons butter, melted
1   tablespoon sugar
½   teaspoon salt
Dash of pepper
2   eggs, lightly beaten

Combine corn and flour. Add remaining ingredients and mix well. Pour into a 2-quart casserole dish and bake in a preheated 350° oven for 45 minutes to 1 hour.

Crock Pot Corn

1   (15-ounce) can kernel corn,
    drained
2   (15-ounce) cans cream-style
    corn
1   (8-ounce) package cream
    cheese, softened
½   cup butter
1   (4-ounce) can chopped green
    chilies, drained

Combine all ingredients in a crock pot and cook on low until well-heated, about 3 hours.

Easy and absolutely delicious - just put in the crock pot and forget about it. May be doubled for a crowd.

Yield: 10 servings.

Aunt Janie's Dressing

8   cups corn bread crumbs
5   cups white bread or biscuit
    crumbs
½   cup minced onion
½   cup chopped celery
1   teaspoon salt
½   teaspoon pepper
2   eggs, beaten
1   teaspoon sage
2   cups, or more, turkey stock
2   large apples, chopped, optional

Combine bread crumbs, celery and onion. Add remaining ingredients and mix well. Place in a greased pan and bake in a preheated 350° oven until brown, about 20 minutes. Makes enough stuffing for a 15-pound turkey.

Aunt Janie's dressing continues to be a favorite passed on from family to family.

Grilled Vegetables with Roasted Garlic Balsamic Vinaigrette

1   summer squash, sliced ¼-inch thick
1   zucchini, sliced ¼-inch thick
1   large red onion, quartered
2   red bell peppers, halved and seeded
2   green bell peppers, halved and seeded
10 medium mushrooms
1   fennel bulb, quartered
1   eggplant, sliced ¼-inch thick
4   tablespoons olive oil
3   tablespoons coarsely chopped fresh oregano
Salt and pepper to taste
Vinaigrette:
3   cloves roasted garlic
4   tablespoons balsamic vinegar
1   tablespoon honey
½   cup olive oil
Salt and pepper to taste

Prepare a charcoal or wood fire and let it burn to embers. Rub vegetables with olive oil and season with salt and pepper. Grill until dark brown, but still crisp. Toss with vinaigrette and place on a platter. Sprinkle with oregano. Let sit 30 minutes at room temperature before serving.

For the Vinaigrette: Combine garlic, vinegar and honey in a blender and puree. With motor running, slowly add oil, drop by drop at first, until emulsified. Season with salt and pepper.

Texas Beans

1   pound pinto beans
1   tablespoon chili powder, or more to taste
1   large onion, chopped
1   can tomatoes
Drippings from 2 slices fried bacon
¼   cup mild picante sauce
Salt

Excellent with barbecue.

Soak, drain and cook beans according to package directions. When done, add remaining ingredients and simmer. Add more chili powder and picante sauce for a hotter dish.

Sweet and Sour Green Beans

1 quart cooked green beans, fresh or frozen
1 medium onion, chopped
8 slices bacon, fried crisp and crumbled
½ cup vinegar
½ cup sugar
½ cup bacon drippings

Layer half beans, onion and bacon in a lightly greased casserole dish. Repeat layers. Combine vinegar, sugar and bacon drippings and pour over casserole. Cook, uncovered, in a preheated 350° oven for 30 minutes.

Good with any meat.

Portobello Mushrooms

¼ cup balsamic vinegar
¾ cup olive oil
Salt and pepper
Fresh chopped garlic
Oregano
Portobello mushrooms

Combine all ingredients except mushrooms and blend well. Pour over mushrooms, cover and refrigerate overnight. Cook mushrooms for five minutes in the oven, on the grill or in the pan. Slice mushrooms diagonally before serving.

This delicious side dish was served with grilled chicken, steamed vegetables, salad and bread at the Doral Golf Resort and Spa in Miami, Florida.

Recipe can be cut in half.

"In cooking, as in all the arts, simplicity is the sign of perfection."
—Curnonsky

Mashed Potato Casserole

8-10 medium boiling potatoes, peeled
Salt and pepper to taste
1   (8-ounce) package cream cheese, softened
2   eggs, lightly beaten
2   tablespoons all-purpose flour
2   tablespoons minced chives or 1 small minced onion
1   can fried onion rings, crumbled

Boil potatoes just until tender. Drain and place in a large bowl. Add salt and pepper to taste and beat well with an electric mixer. Add cream cheese and beat until well blended. Add eggs, flour and onion and mix well. Correct seasonings and turn into a buttered casserole. Top with onion rings and bake, uncovered, in a preheated 325° oven until puffy and golden.

Yield: 6 to 8 servings.

Potato Gourmet

6-8 medium Idaho potatoes
2   cups shredded sharp Cheddar cheese
6   tablespoons margarine, divided
1½ cups sour cream
3   green onions, chopped
1   teaspoon salt
¼   teaspoon pepper

Boil unpeeled potatoes until tender. Cool, peel and shred with a grater. Combine cheese and 4 tablespoons margarine in a saucepan. Heat, stirring, until cheese is almost melted. Remove from heat and blend in sour cream, onion, salt and pepper. Fold in potatoes and turn into a greased casserole dish. Dot with remaining margarine and bake in a preheated 300° oven for 25 minutes.

Yield: 6 to 8 servings.

"We do not remember days, we remember moments."
—Cesare Pavese

Potato Pancakes

3 cups grated raw potatoes
1 cup grated onion
2 teaspoons salt
Dash of pepper
3 tablespoons all-purpose flour
2 eggs, well beaten
1 teaspoon sugar
¼ teaspoon baking powder

A good accompaniment to fried fish or pork chops.

Combine potatoes and onion. Add remaining ingredients and blend well. Drop mixture by spoonfuls onto a hot, well-greased griddle. Fry on both sides until brown. Serve crispy hot with applesauce.

Julia Child's Red Potatoes and Onions

20 small red new potatoes, well washed
4 tablespoons olive oil, divided
6 medium red onions, peeled and cut crosswise into ½-inch slices
1 tablespoon red wine vinegar
1 tablespoon white wine
Coarse (kosher) salt to taste
Butcher-grind black pepper to taste
5 tablespoons chopped Italian parsley, divided

Garden greats on the grill. Use this technique for other vegetables too - tomatoes, red and yellow peppers, zucchini, eggplant or summer squash.

Preheat oven to 350°. Prick potatoes with a fork and bake in shallow roasting pan 45 to 50 minutes. Remove. Coat potatoes with 1 tablespoon olive oil and thread on thin skewers. Place on grill over very hot coals and cook, turning once, until browned and tender, 1 to 2 minutes. Remove from grill. Brush one side of onion slices with 1 tablespoon olive oil and place, oiled-side down, on grill over very hot coals. Cook until brown and just tender, 2 to 4 minutes. Do not overcook. Remove from grill with spatula and reserve. Remove potatoes from skewers, cut in half and place in a bowl. Carefully toss with remaining olive oil, vinegar, wine, salt, pepper and 4 tablespoons parsley. Arrange potatoes in center of platter. Surround with grilled onion slices. Sprinkle salt, pepper and remaining parsley over onion slices. Serve at room temperature.

Yield: 4 servings.

New Potatoes with Lemon Horseradish Sauce

1-2 pounds new potatoes
1/4 cup butter
1/2 teaspoon salt
1/4 teaspoon pepper
2 teaspoons lemon juice
1 tablespoon prepared horseradish
2 tablespoons chopped fresh parsley

Peel a 1/2-inch strip around center of each potato. Melt butter in a 2-quart baking dish. Add salt, pepper, lemon juice and horseradish. Stir in potatoes until well-coated. Cover and bake in a preheated 350° oven until potatoes are tender, about 1 hour. Garnish with parsley.

Oven Potatoes

1/4 cup margarine, melted
1 tablespoon grated onion
1 tablespoon chopped parsley
1/2 teaspoon dried thyme leaves
1/2 teaspoon salt
1/8 teaspoon pepper
4 large unpeeled potatoes, thinly sliced
1 1/2 cups grated Cheddar cheese

Combine margarine, onion, parsley, thyme, salt and pepper. Layer potatoes in a lightly greased 9 x 13-inch baking dish, brushing each layer with butter mixture. Bake in a pre-heated 425° oven until potatoes are tender, about 40 minutes. Sprinkle with cheese and continue baking until cheese melts, about 5 more minutes.

Yield: 6 servings.

Onion Casserole

Sliced onions
Crushed potato chips
Grated Cheddar cheese
1 can cream of mushroom soup
1/2 cup milk

Layer onions, chips and cheese in a greased casserole dish. Combine soup and milk and pour over casserole. Bake, covered, in a pre-heated 350° oven for 20 minutes. Remove cover and bake 10 more minutes.

McDonald Boys' Rice

2 cups long-grain rice
4¼ cups water
1 teaspoon salt
6 tablespoons butter, divided
½ Vidalia or sweet onion, chopped
1 red bell pepper, chopped
3 tablespoons parsley
2 teaspoons pepper
1½ teaspoons seasoned salt

Great with all grilled meats.

Place rice, water, salt and 2 tablespoons butter in a saucepan. Bring to boil, cover, reduce heat and simmer until cooked, about 20 minutes. Remove from heat, leaving covered, and cool. Melt remaining butter in a large skillet and sauté onions until tender. Add red pepper and sauté to desired tenderness. Add rice and remaining ingredients and stir.

Yield: 8 servings.

Brown Rice Casserole

½ cup margarine, melted
1 cup uncooked rice
1 (10-ounce) can French onion soup
1 (10-ounce) can beef consommé
1 (4-ounce) can sliced mushrooms, drained

Combine all ingredients in a large bowl and mix well. Spoon into a buttered 1¾-quart baking dish and bake, covered, in a preheated 350° oven for 1 hour.

Yield: 6 servings.

Squash Delight

1 pound squash, chopped
½ pound bulk pork sausage, cooked and crumbled
½ cup mayonnaise
¼ cup chopped green bell pepper
1 egg, lightly beaten
1 teaspoon sugar
1 cup grated Cheddar cheese, divided
½ cup bread crumbs

Boil squash until tender, drain thoroughly and mash. Combine sausage, mayonnaise, bell pepper, egg, sugar and ¾ cup cheese. Add squash and stir well. Pour into a greased 2-quart casserole dish and top with bread crumbs and remaining cheese. Bake in a preheated 350° oven for 40 minutes.

Yield: 6 to 8 servings.

Summer Squash Casserole

2   pounds summer squash,
     sliced
1   medium onion, sliced
¾   cup mayonnaise
1   cup grated Cheddar cheese
Salt and pepper to taste
¾   cup herb-seasoned stuffing
     mix

Boil squash and onion in water until tender, about 10 minutes. Drain and mix with mayonnaise, cheese and salt and pepper. Turn into a buttered 1½-quart casserole and sprinkle with stuffing mix. Bake in a preheated 350° oven, uncovered, for 30 minutes.

Yield: 6 servings.

Sweet Potato Casserole

3   cups cooked, mashed sweet
     potatoes
1   cup sugar
½   cup butter, softened
1   teaspoon vanilla
2   eggs, lightly beaten
⅓   cup milk
⅔   cup firmly packed brown sugar
1   cup flour
1   cup chopped pecans
⅓   cup butter, melted

Combine sweet potatoes, sugar, butter, vanilla, eggs and milk and blend thoroughly. Turn into a 12-inch baking dish. Combine brown sugar, flour and pecans and spread over sweet potato mixture. Drizzle with melted butter and bake in a preheated 350° oven for 30 minutes.

Yield: 8 to 10 servings.

"Year by year the complexities of this spinning world grow more bewildering and so each year we need all the more to seek peace and comfort in the joyful simplicities."
—Woman's Home Companion, December 1935

Breaded Tomatoes

4 cups canned or mashed tomatoes, squeezed dry
½ cup vegetable oil
1 teaspoon salt
¼ teaspoon pepper
½ cup chopped onion
½ teaspoon charcoal seasoning
2 tablespoons butter
2 tablespoons flour
½ cup sugar
3 slices white bread

Combine tomatoes, oil, onion, salt, pepper and charcoal seasoning in a large skillet. Bring to a boil over medium heat. While tomato mixture is cooking, melt butter and stir in flour, mixing thoroughly. Add to tomato mixture and continue cooking until thickened, stirring constantly. Add sugar, reduce heat and simmer 2 to 3 minutes. Toast bread and cut into squares. Add to tomato mixture just before serving.

Yield: 6 servings.

"It's difficult to think anything but pleasant thoughts while eating a home-grown tomato."
—Lewis Grizzard

Macaroni and Tomato Casserole

1 cup uncooked macaroni
⅓ cup chopped onion
⅓ cup chopped green bell pepper
⅓ cup chopped celery
¼ cup margarine
1 (10-ounce) can cream of mushroom soup
1 (15-ounce) can tomatoes, drained
1 cup shredded Cheddar cheese, divided
Dash of pepper

Cook macaroni according to package directions and drain. Sauté onion, bell pepper and celery in margarine. Stir in macaroni, soup, tomatoes, ½ cup cheese and pepper. Pour into a greased 2-quart casserole and sprinkle with remaining cheese. Bake in a preheated 350° oven 25 to 30 minutes.

Yield: 8 to 10 servings.

Tomatoes Stuffed with Broccoli

6   medium tomatoes
1   (10-ounce) package frozen
     chopped broccoli
1   cup shredded Swiss cheese
1   cup soft bread crumbs
½   cup mayonnaise
2   tablespoons chopped onion
2   tablespoons grated Parmesan
     cheese

Slice off tops of tomatoes and scoop out insides, leaving a thick shell intact. Sprinkle insides with salt and pepper and invert on a wire rack to drain for 30 minutes. Cook broccoli according to package directions, omitting salt. Drain well and combine with Swiss cheese, bread crumbs, mayonnaise and onion. Stuff into tomato shells and sprinkle with Parmesan cheese. Bake in a preheated 350° oven for 30 minutes.

Yield: 6 servings.

Vidalia Onion Casserole

4   large Vidalia onions, sliced
¼   cup unsalted butter
1½   sleeves round buttery
     crackers, crushed
¼   cup unsalted butter, softened
8   ounces Cheddar cheese,
     shredded
Salt, pepper and paprika to taste
3   large eggs, beaten
1   cup milk

Sauté onion rings in ¼ cup butter in a skillet. Combine cracker crumbs with ¼ cup butter in a bowl and mix thoroughly. Spread crumb mixture in a greased 9 x 13-inch casserole dish, reserving ¼ cup. Layer onion rings over crumbs and sprinkle with cheese. Season with salt, pepper and paprika. Combine eggs and milk in a bowl and blend well. Pour over onion rings and sprinkle with reserved crumbs. Bake in a preheated 350° oven until heated through and onions are tender, 35 to 40 minutes.

Yield: 8 servings.

Entrées

Elegant Beef Tenderloin

1   (6-pound) beef tenderloin,
    trimmed
1   cup cream sherry
1   cup olive oil
1   cup soy sauce
1   clove garlic, minced
Freshly ground pepper to taste

Place beef in a shallow baking dish. Combine remaining ingredients and pour over beef. Turn to coat, cover and marinate 8 hours, turning occasionally. Bake uncovered in a preheated 425° oven, 20 minutes for medium rare, or grill over hot coals until desired degree of doneness.

Yield: 18 servings.

Seasoned Brisket

Brisket
Salt
Garlic salt
Celery salt
2   teaspoons sugar
Worcestershire sauce
Liquid smoke

As good cold as it is warm.

Rub meat on all sides with remaining ingredients. Wrap in foil and refrigerate overnight in a tightly covered pan. The next day, season again with the same ingredients except sugar. Wrap in foil and bake in a preheated 250° oven one hour per pound of meat. Open foil and pour off grease. Serve with a sauce of sour cream and horseradish or serve with barbecue sauce.

Beef Tips

1   (2½ to 3-pound) round
    steak, cut in cubes
1   can French onion soup
1   can cream of mushroom
    soup

Easy Sunday dinner — just put in oven before church.

Place meat in a 3-quart baking dish. Pour soups over and stir to mix. Cover with foil and bake in a preheated 300° oven until tender, 2½ to 3 hours. Serve over noodles, rice or creamed potatoes.

Yield: 6 to 8 servings.

London Broil

½ cup canola oil
¾ cup soy sauce
¼ cup Worcestershire sauce
2 tablespoons dry mustard
2¼ teaspoons salt
1 teaspoon pepper
½ cup wine vinegar
1½ teaspoons parsley flakes
2 cloves garlic, minced
⅓ cup fresh lemon juice
1 (4-pound) flank steak

Combine all ingredients except meat and mix well. Place meat in a marinade dish and cover with marinade. Refrigerate 3 to 6 hours, turning container occasionally. Preheat grill to medium. Drain marinade into a saucepan and bring to a boil. Reduce heat and keep warm. Grill meat 8 to 10 minutes per side. Meat should be very pink in center. Remove from heat and place on a sturdy cutting board. Slice thinly on the diagonal and arrange over hot French bread. Drizzle with hot marinade. Serve with fresh garden salad, grilled vegetables or corn on the cob.

Yield: 8 servings.

Pepper Steak

1 pound round steak, cut in strips
2 tablespoons vegetable oil
½ cup chopped onion
2 teaspoons garlic juice
1 teaspoon salt
1 beef bouillon cube
1 cup hot water
2 tablespoons soy sauce
2 cups cooked tomatoes
1 large green bell pepper, cut in strips
2 tablespoons cornstarch
¼ cup cold water
1 can chop suey vegetables, drained

Brown meat in oil. Add onions, garlic juice and salt. Dissolve bouillon cube in hot water and add to meat along with soy sauce. Cover, reduce heat and simmer 20 to 30 minutes. Mash tomatoes and heat with pepper strips. Add to meat and cook 10 minutes. Dissolve cornstarch in cold water and add to meat to thicken. Add vegetables and simmer 5 minutes, stirring constantly. Serve over rice or chow mein noodles.

Yield: 4 servings.

Rouladen

4 slices beef sirloin tip
Salt and pepper to taste
Prepared mustard
4 slices bacon
1 dill pickle, sliced
2 medium onions, chopped
Butter
1 cup water
Flour

Have butcher slice beef ¼-inch thick and about the size of a salad plate. Sprinkle with salt and pepper and spread with mustard. Place bacon strips and pickles on meat and cover with onions. Roll up jelly-roll style and fasten with tooth picks. Melt butter in a skillet and brown meat on all sides. Add water, bring to a boil, reduce heat, cover and simmer until tender, about 45 minutes. Remove meat and thicken gravy with flour.

Serve with red cabbage and potato dumplings.

Yield: 2 servings.

Grilled Pineapple Burgers

2 pounds lean ground beef
3 tablespoons Italian dressing
1 teaspoon salt
⅛ teaspoon pepper
1 (15¼-ounce) can sliced pineapple, drained
8 slices bacon
¾ cup barbecue sauce
¼ cup firmly packed brown sugar
¼ cup honey
1 tablespoon lemon juice

Mix ground beef, salad dressing and salt and pepper. Shape into 8 patties, 3 inches in diameter. Press a pineapple slice into each patty, wrap with a bacon slice and secure with a toothpick. Combine barbecue sauce, brown sugar, honey and lemon juice. Place patties in a glass or plastic dish and cover with barbecue mixture. Cover and refrigerate at least 2 hours. Grill patties pineapple-side down 4 inches from hot coals for 12 to 15 minutes. Turn and brush with marinade. Grill 10 to 15 minutes more. Heat remaining marinade and serve with patties.

Yield: 8 servings.

Stuffed Peppers

8 green bell peppers
2 pounds ground chuck
1 large onion, minced
1 teaspoon garlic salt
½ teaspoon black pepper
10 ounces grated Cheddar cheese, divided
1 (16-ounce) carton sour cream

Parboil peppers in a large pan. Drain, cut in half and remove seeds. Set aside. Brown ground beef and onion. Drain and add garlic salt, pepper and half of cheese. Stir in sour cream and mix well. Stuff peppers with beef mixture and place in a 9 x 13-inch baking pan. Top with remaining cheese and bake in a preheated 350° oven for 30 minutes.

Yield: 8 servings.

Tortilla Chip Bake

2 pounds ground chuck
1 medium onion, chopped
1 (10-ounce) can chopped tomatoes with green chilies
2 (16-ounce) cans chili beans
1 (10-ounce) can cream of mushroom soup
Salt and pepper to taste
1 (12-ounce) package tortilla chips, crushed
8 ounces process cheese, shredded

Brown beef with onion in a skillet, stirring until crumbly. Drain well and add tomatoes, beans, soup, salt and pepper. Mix well. Layer tortilla chips and beef mixture in a 9 x 13-inch baking dish. Bake in a preheated 350° oven for 30 minutes. Sprinkle with cheese and continue baking until cheese melts.

Yield: 8 servings.

Meat Loaf

1 pound ground chuck
1 medium onion, chopped
1 small green bell pepper, chopped
½ cup oats
2 eggs, lightly beaten
½ cup milk
¾ cup ketchup
1 can cream of chicken soup
1 can cream of celery soup
½ soup can water

Place beef, onion, bell pepper, oats, eggs and milk in a large bowl and lightly mix. Add ketchup and shape into loaf. Bake, uncovered in a preheated 350° oven until almost done, about 30 minutes. Drain off any drippings. Combine soups and water and pour over meat. Cook until done.

Yield: 6 servings.

Taco Pie

1 pound ground chuck
1 package taco seasoning mix
1 (16-ounce) can refried beans
2 cups shredded Cheddar cheese, divided
1 cup crushed corn chips
1 medium onion, chopped
¾ cup water
1 (8-ounce) jar taco sauce, divided
1 baked 9-inch pie crust
Sour cream
Shredded lettuce
Chopped tomato

Brown meat and onion and drain well. Add taco seasoning and water and stir well. Bring to a boil, reduce heat and simmer for 20 minutes. Combine refried beans and ⅓ cup taco sauce. Spread half of bean mixture over pie crust. Top with half of meat mixture, half of cheese and all of corn chips. Repeat layering with remaining bean mixture, meat and cheese. Bake in a preheated 400° oven for 20 to 25 minutes. Serve topped with sour cream, lettuce and tomato.,

Yield: 10 servings.

Enchilada Casserole

1 pound ground chuck
1 (20-ounce) jar thick and chunky salsa
1 large onion, chopped
2 cans refried beans
½ teaspoon garlic powder
½ tablespoon chili powder
½ teaspoon salt
1 cup all-purpose flour
1 cup water
6 tortillas
2 (8-ounce) packages Mexican-style grated cheese

Brown beef and drain well. Place salsa, onion, beans, garlic powder, chili powder, salt , flour and water in a large saucepan. Heat, stirring, until well-blended. Add beef. Place 3 tortillas in bottom of a 9 x 13-inch baking dish. Pour half of beef mixture over top. Sprinkle with half of cheese. Bake in a preheated 350° oven until cheese melts, then repeat layers. Continue baking 30 more minutes.

Yield: 8 servings.

"Pleasure is the beginning and the end of living happily."
—Epicurus

Shrimp Fettuccine

5	green onions, chopped
2	cups sliced mushrooms
2	cloves garlic, minced
½	cup butter, divided
2	tablespoons vegetable oil
1	pound peeled, raw shrimp
2	teaspoons salt
8	ounces fettuccine
¾	cup grated Romano cheese
¾	cup grated Parmesan cheese
1	cup whipping cream
½	cup chopped fresh parsley

Sauté onions, mushrooms and garlic in ¼ cup butter and oil in a large skillet. Add shrimp and sauté until pink. Pour off excess liquid and season with salt. Cover and keep warm. Cook noodles in salted, boiling water according to package directions. Drain. Melt remaining butter in a saucepan. Add noodles, cheese and cream. Mix well and combine with shrimp mixture. Sprinkle with parsley, toss and serve immediately.

Yield: 4 to 6 servings.

Shrimp Casserole

2	large eggs
1	cup evaporated milk
1	cup plain yogurt
8	ounces Feta cheese, crumbled
½	pound Swiss cheese, shredded
⅓	cup chopped fresh parsley
1	teaspoon dried basil
1	teaspoon dried oregano
4	cloves garlic, minced
½	pound angel hair pasta, cooked
1	(16-ounce) jar mild chunky salsa
1	pound peeled raw medium shrimp
½	pound mozzarella cheese, shredded

Blend eggs, milk, yogurt, Feta, Swiss cheese, parsley, basil, oregano and garlic in a large bowl. Spread half of pasta over bottom of a 9 x 12-inch baking dish which has been coated with nonstick spray. Top with salsa and half of shrimp. Cover with remaining pasta. Pour egg mixture over pasta and top with remaining shrimp. Sprinkle with mozzarella cheese and bake in a preheated 350° oven for 30 minutes. Remove and let stand for 10 minutes before serving.

A big hit at dinner parties served with green salad and baked apples.

Yield: 10 servings.

Jambalaya

2 cans French onion soup
2 cans cream of celery soup
1 large jar sliced mushrooms, undrained
1 can tomatoes and green chilies
1 cup chopped onion
1 green bell pepper, chopped
3 green onions, chopped
2 pounds smoked sausage, sliced
2 pounds peeled raw shrimp
2 cups uncooked converted rice

Combine all ingredients in a large dish and cover tightly with foil. Bake in a preheated 350° for 1 to 1½ hours.

Yield: 10 to 12 servings.

Shrimp Destin

¼ cup chopped scallions or green onions
2 teaspoons minced garlic
1 cup butter or margarine
2 pounds raw peeled, deveined large shrimp
1 teaspoon lemon juice
1 tablespoon white wine
¼ teaspoon salt
Coarsely ground black pepper
1 teaspoon dried dill
1 teaspoon chopped fresh parsley
3 French rolls, split lengthwise and toasted

Sauté scallions and garlic in butter until scallions are tender. Add shrimp, lemon juice, wine, salt and pepper and cook over medium heat about 5 minutes, stirring occasionally. Stir in dill and parsley. Spoon over rolls and serve immediately.

Yield: 6 servings.

"Only the heart knows how to find what is precious."
—Dostoevsky

Barbecued Shrimp

½ pound margarine
1 cup olive oil
8 ounces chili sauce
3 tablespoons Worcestershire sauce
2 lemons, sliced
4 cloves garlic, chopped
3 tablespoons lemon juice
1 ½ tablespoons liquid smoke
1 tablespoon parsley
1 teaspoon hot pepper sauce
2 teaspoons paprika
2 teaspoons oregano
2 teaspoons cayenne pepper
Salt and pepper to taste
8 pounds raw unpeeled extra-large shrimp, rinsed

Combine all ingredients except shrimp in a large saucepan. Cook over low heat, stirring occasionally, until well blended, about 10 minutes. Place shrimp in a large shallow pan. Pour sauce over shrimp and cook, uncovered, in a preheated 325° over for 30 to 40 minutes, basting frequently. Serve with a fresh garden salad and plenty of hot French bread for sopping up the juice.

Recipe may be halved.

Yield: 14 servings.

A great informal dinner for the beach house or back porch. Don't hesitate to spread newspapers and stock up on paper napkins. (The juice will ruin your good linens!) Dig in and enjoy the compliments of the crowd.

Dill Salmon Cakes

1 large can salmon, deboned and drained
1 bunch green onions, chopped
1 small green bell pepper, chopped
1 (8-ounce) container sour cream
1 teaspoon dried dill
1 teaspoon garlic powder
3 tablespoons lemon juice
½-1 cup stuffing mix

Combine all ingredients in a large bowl. Shape into cakes and refrigerate or freeze until set, 1 to 2 hours. (This helps prevent cakes from separating when cooking.) Brown on both sides in a small amount of oil in a nonstick skillet. Serve with tartar sauce.

Note: To serve as appetizer, shape into small cakes.

Simply Delicious Crab Cakes

2 (4½-ounce) cans fancy lump crab meat
2 tablespoons capers
2 tablespoons chopped scallions
3 tablespoons white wine
Cayenne pepper to taste
1 egg, lightly beaten
3 tablespoons flour
3 tablespoons butter or olive oil

Combine all ingredients except butter in order listed and form into 4 cakes. Sauté in melted butter until lightly browned, about 4 minutes on each side. Serve with lemon wedges.

Yield: 4 servings.

Ham and Asparagus Crêpes

2 tablespoons minced onion
3 tablespoons butter or margarine
½ teaspoon salt
⅛ teaspoon cayenne
¾ cup milk
1 cup whipping cream, divided
1½ cups diced ham
1 (10-ounce) package frozen asparagus spears, thawed, or 1 can, drained
½ cup mayonnaise
8 crêpes
Paprika

Sauté onion in butter for 2 minutes. Stir in flour, salt and cayenne and cook, stirring constantly, until thick and bubbly. Stir in milk and ¾ cup whipping cream. Continue cooking until thickened and bubbling, about 1 minute. Remove ¼ cup sauce for topping. Add ham to remaining sauce. Lay out crêpes and spread about ¼ cup filling on each. Top with 2 to 3 asparagus spears, roll up and place seam-side down on a buttered baking sheet. Whip remaining cream, stir in reserved sauce and mayonnaise and spread over crepes. Sprinkle with paprika and bake in a preheated 350° oven for 25 minutes.

Yield: 4 servings.
Covington's

Chalupas

1	(3-pound) pork roast
1	pound pinto beans
2	cloves garlic
2	tablespoons chili powder
1	tablespoon ground cumin
1	teaspoon oregano
1	(7-ounce) can chopped green chilies
1	tablespoon salt

Cut roast into 3 pieces and place in a crock pot. Add remaining ingredients and enough water to barely cover. Cook on medium 8 hours or overnight. If beans are still underdone, remove cover, turn to high heat and cook several hours longer. If too thick, more hot water can be added. When roast is tender and bean are done, shred pork and serve on crisp-fried tortillas, topped with cheese, lettuce, onions, tomatoes and picante sauce.

Yield: 8 servings.

Sweet and Sour Pork

1½	pounds boneless pork, cut into strips
2	tablespoons vegetable oil
1	(13¼-ounce) can pineapple chunks, drained and juice reserved
⅓	cup vinegar
2	tablespoons soy sauce
¼	cup firmly packed brown sugar
1	carrot, cut into ¼-inch bias slices
1	(1-pound) can bean sprouts, drained
1	onion, sliced
1	green bell pepper, cut into strips
3	tablespoons cornstarch
¼	cup water
1	teaspoon ginger
Hot cooked rice	

Brown pork in hot oil in a skillet. Add enough water to reserved pineapple syrup to make 1¼ cups. Pour over pork and add vinegar, soy sauce and brown sugar. Bring to a boil, reduce heat, cover and simmer 45 minutes. Add carrots and cook 2 more minutes. Add pineapple, bean sprouts, onion and bell pepper. Cover and cook 10 minutes. Blend cornstarch, ginger and water. Stir until cornstarch is dissolved and add to pork. Cook, stirring, until sauce is thickened and bubbly. Serve over rice.

Yield: 6 servings.

Bacon and Broccoli Stir Fried Rice

10 strips bacon
1 egg, lightly beaten
1 bunch green onions, chopped
1 bunch fresh broccoli, chopped
2 tablespoons soy sauce
4 cups cooked rice

Cook bacon until crisp, remove and reserve 2 tablespoons drippings. Drain bacon and crumble. Cook egg and onions in reserved drippings until done. Add broccoli and soy sauce and cook over medium heat until broccoli is crisp tender, 2 to 3 minutes. Stir in bacon and rice.

Yield 6 to 8 servings.

A Simple Pleasure...

The politeness of a child to an elderly person when it's natural rather than dutiful.

Chicken Rhodo

1 tablespoon parsley flakes
2 teaspoons garlic salt
2 teaspoons lemon pepper
1 teaspoon oregano
2 tablespoons Worcestershire sauce
½ cup Italian dressing
Juice of 1 lemon
Cracked pepper to taste
8 chicken breasts

Combine all ingredients except chicken and blend well. Pour over chicken, cover and refrigerate at least 2 hours, turning often. Preheat grill to medium. Drain chicken, reserving marinade. Place chicken on one side of grill away from coals. Close grill, cover and cook 30 minutes. Place chicken over low coals and cook 30 minutes more, basting frequently and turning carefully.

Yield: 8 servings.

This is a tasty and easy way to grill chicken because the first cooking time requires no attention. The ingredients are usually on hand, so what could be simpler?

Red Beans and Rice

1	pound dried red beans
1	large ham bone
1	large onion, chopped
1	large clove garlic, chopped
1	bay leaf
⅛	teaspoon cayenne pepper, or more to taste
2	teaspoons salt
1	pound smoked mild or hot link sausage, cut into 2-inch pieces

Hot cooked rice

Wash beans thoroughly, cover with water and soak overnight. Drain and place in a heavy saucepan. Cover with water and add ham bone, onion, garlic, bay leaf and red pepper. Bring to a boil, reduce heat, cover and simmer until beans are tender, about 2 hours. Add more water during cooking, if necessary. Add salt and sausage and simmer, uncovered, until a thick gravy forms, stirring occasionally. Remove bay leaf before serving. Serve over hot cooked rice.

Yield: 4 servings.

Sausage Potato Bake

1	pound bulk pork sausage
1	(10¾-ounce) can cream of celery soup
⅓	cup milk
½	cup chopped onion
1	small jar pimento, drained
½	teaspoon salt
¼	teaspoon pepper
4	cups thinly sliced potatoes
1	cup shredded Cheddar cheese

Cook sausage in a skillet, stirring to crumble, until brown. Drain. Combine soup, milk, onion, pimento, salt and pepper in a bowl. Layer half of potatoes in a 2 quart casserole. Top with half of sauce and half of soup mixture. Repeat layers. Cover and bake in a preheated 350° oven until potatoes are tender, about 1 hour. Sprinkle with cheese and bake, uncovered, 15 more minutes.

Yield: 6 servings.

"Take the gentle path."
—George Herbert

Tropical Shrimp Kabobs

1 pound fresh raw, peeled and deveined shrimp
16 cantaloupe cubes
16 honeydew melon cubes
16 green bell pepper pieces
3 tablespoons honey
4 teaspoons teriyaki sauce
1 teaspoon lemon juice

Thread shrimp, melon cubes and bell pepper on eight skewers. Combine remaining ingredients in a small bowl. Place skewers on an oiled grill rack over hot coals and brush with sauce. Cook 8 to 10 minutes, turning twice and basting frequently, until shrimp turns pink.

Serve with rice, grilled pineapple slices and Frozen Lime Tarts for a refreshing low-fat meal on a hot summer evening.

Yield: 4 to 6 servings.

Key Lime Grilled Dill Chicken

8 chicken breasts, skinned and boned
½ cup lime juice
⅓ cup olive oil
4 green onions, chopped
4 cloves garlic, minced
3 tablespoons chopped fresh dill, divided
¼ teaspoon pepper

Flatten chicken breasts. Combine lime juice, oil, onion, garlic, 2 tablespoons dill and pepper in a zip-lock plastic bag. Add chicken and refrigerate 2 to 4 hours, turning occasionally. Drain chicken and discard marinade. Grill over medium-hot coals until tender and juices run clear, about 6 minutes per side. Sprinkle with remaining dill before serving.

Yield: 8 servings.

Sesame Chicken Kabobs

¼ cup soy sauce
¼-½ cup Russian salad dressing
1-2 tablespoons sesame seeds
2 tablespoons lemon juice
¼ teaspoon garlic powder
¼ teaspoon ground ginger
4 boneless chicken breasts, cut into 1-inch cubes

Combine all ingredients except chicken. Pour over chicken, cover and refrigerate overnight or at least six hours. Drain chicken and thread onto skewers. Grill over low heat until done, about 12 minutes.

Yield: 4 servings.

Southwestern Grilled Chicken

2   medium tomatoes, quartered
2   cups chopped onion
½   cup chopped red bell pepper
4   cloves garlic, minced
¼   cup fresh cilantro leaves
⅔   cup soy sauce
6   tablespoons vegetable oil
2   tablespoons fresh lime juice
1½ teaspoons pepper
8   boneless chicken breasts
Chopped fresh parsley

Place all ingredients except chicken and parsley in a blender or food processor and pulse until blended. Pour over chicken, cover and refrigerate 4 to 12 hours, turning frequently. Remove chicken from marinade, reserving marinade. Grill chicken over medium coals for 20 to 30 minutes, turning frequently and basting with reserved marinade. Sprinkle with parsley before serving.

Yield: 8 servings.

Marinated Pork Tenderloin

1   (2½ to 3-pound) pork
    tenderloin
½   cup soy sauce
¼   cup chopped green onions
2   cloves garlic, minced
1   teaspoon ginger
2   teaspoons pepper
¼   cup sesame seeds

Place tenderloin in a zip-lock bag. Combine remaining ingredients and pour into bag. Seal and refrigerate overnight, turning occasionally. Cook slowly on a grill.

Italian Pork Tenderloin

1   package zesty Italian dressing
    mix
Balsamic vinegar
Pork tenderloins
Salt and pepper

The slow cooking makes the smoke-flavored pork melt in your mouth.

Prepare salad dressing according to package directions, substituting balsamic vinegar. Rinse pork in cool water and drain. Season with salt and pepper and place in a zip-lock plastic bag. Pour dressing over pork, seal and refrigerate for 2 hours, turning occasionally. Drain pork, reserving marinade. Grill tenderloins slowly over low to medium heat, basting frequently with marinade, for 1 hour, or until meat is no longer pink.

Country Captain

12 chicken pieces (6 breasts, 3 drumsticks, 3 thighs
Salt and pepper
½ cup flour
1 tablespoon paprika
1 cup butter, divided
1 large onion, chopped
1 large green bell pepper, chopped
1 clove garlic, chopped
½ cup butter
1 (16-ounce) can tomatoes
¼ cup chopped fresh parsley
2 teaspoons vinegar
2 tablespoons prepared mustard
1 tablespoon Worcestershire sauce
1 teaspoon curry powder
1 teaspoon thyme
1 teaspoon salt
1 teaspoon pepper
1 (4-ounce) can mushrooms, drained
1 cup currants
½ cup toasted slivered almonds, or more to taste

Wash and pat chicken dry with paper towels. Sprinkle with salt and pepper and dredge in flour mixed with paprika. Melt ½ cup butter in a skillet and brown chicken. Arrange in an oblong baking dish. Sauté onion, green pepper and garlic in remaining butter until onions are transparent but not brown. Add tomatoes, parsley, vinegar, mustard, Worcestershire sauce, curry, thyme, salt and pepper and simmer about 20 minutes. Add mushrooms and pour over chicken. Cover tightly with foil and bake in a preheated 350° oven for 1 hour and 15 minutes. Lift foil and sprinkle currants over chicken. Cover and bake another 15 minutes. Transfer chicken to a serving dish, leaving currants on top. Pour sauce all around chicken and top with slivered almonds. Serve with rice.

Yield: 6 servings.

Note: Boned, skinless chicken breasts cut into pieces may be substituted for chicken pieces. This dish is ideal for a football buffet.

"No one who cooks cooks alone. Even at her most solitary, a cook in the kitchen is surrounded by generations of cooks past, the advice and menus of cooks present, the wisdom of cookbook writers."
—Laurie Colwin

Chicken Crescent Rollups

1 (3-ounce) package cream cheese, softened
2 tablespoons butter
½ teaspoon lemon pepper
1 (8-ounce) can chopped mushrooms, drained
2 boneless chicken breasts, cooked and chopped
1 can refrigerated crescent rolls
Melted butter
Seasoned bread crumbs
Chopped walnuts

Combine cream cheese, butter, lemon pepper, mushrooms and chicken. Divide rolls along perforations. Place 1 heaping tablespoon chicken mixture on each roll, fold over and pinch edges closed. Brush with melted butter and sprinkle with bread crumbs and nuts. Bake on a cookie sheet in a preheated 375° oven until brown, 15 to 20 minutes.

"I have learned, in whatsoever state I am, therewith to be content."
—St. Paul

Chicken Cordon Bleu

6 skinless boneless chicken breasts
1 (8-ounce) package Swiss cheese slices
1 (8-ounce) package sliced cooked ham
3 tablespoons all-purpose flour
1 teaspoon paprika
6 tablespoons butter or margarine
½ cup dry white wine
1 chicken bouillon cube
1 tablespoon cornstarch
1 cup whipping cream

Flatten chicken breasts and fold cheese and ham slices to fit on top. Fold breasts over filling and fasten edges with toothpicks. Dredge chicken in flour mixed with paprika. Melt butter in a 12-inch skillet and brown chicken on all sides. Add wine and bouillon, reduce heat to low, cover and simmer until chicken is fork-tender, about 30 minutes. Transfer chicken to serving dish and remove toothpicks. Blend cornstarch in whipping cream until smooth. Gradually stir into skillet. Cook, stirring constantly, until thickened and serve over chicken.

Yield: 6 servings.

Santa Fe Chicken

1¼ pounds boneless skinless chicken breasts
1 teaspoon paprika
1 teaspoon salt
¼ teaspoon pepper
1 teaspoon olive oil
1 medium onion, chopped
1 clove garlic, chopped
1 small green bell pepper, chopped
1 can tomatoes and green chilies
Chicken broth
1½ cups instant rice
¾ cup Monterey Jack cheese

Cut chicken into thin strips and sprinkle with paprika, salt and pepper. Heat oil in a skillet over medium-high heat. Cook chicken for 2 minutes. Add onion, garlic and green pepper and cook until tender, about 4 minutes. Drain tomatoes and reserve liquid. Add enough chicken broth to tomato liquid to make 1½ cups. Add to skillet and bring to a boil. Stir in rice and tomatoes. Cover and remove from heat. Let stand until all liquid is absorbed, about 5 minutes. Sprinkle with cheese and serve.

Yield: 6 servings.

Italian Chicken Parmesan

6 boneless chicken breasts
1 egg, beaten
1 cup seasoned Italian bread crumbs
½ cup grated Parmesan cheese
Juice of ½ lemon
½ cup butter or margarine, melted

Flatten chicken breasts with a rolling pin. Dip in egg, then in mixture of bread crumbs and cheese. Lay in a greased 9 x 13-inch baking dish and drizzle with mixture of butter and lemon juice. Bake in a preheated 350° oven for 20 minutes. Turn and continue baking until golden brown, 15 to 20 minutes more.

Easy enough to prepare even after a hard day of work.

Yield 6 servings.

A Simple Pleasure...
The generosity and hospitality of good neighbors.
—Sarah Ban Breathnach

Sweet and Sour Chicken

¼ cup firmly packed light
   brown sugar
2 tablespoons cornstarch
½ teaspoon salt
¼ cup vinegar
1 tablespoon soy sauce
1 (13¼-ounce) can pineapple
   tidbits
1 cup green bell pepper strips
¼ cup thinly sliced onion
6 tablespoons margarine
1 (2½ to 3-pound) chicken, cut
   up
Hot cooked rice

Combine sugar, cornstarch and salt in a bowl. Gradually add vinegar, then soy sauce, pineapple with syrup, green pepper and onion. Set aside. Melt margarine in a large skillet. Add chicken pieces and brown on all sides. Reduce heat, cover and simmer until tender, 30 to 40 minutes. Remove chicken from skillet and add pineapple mixture. Cook over medium heat, stirring constantly, until thickened. Return chicken to skillet, reduce heat, cover and simmer 5 to 10 minutes. Place rice on a serving platter and top with chicken and sauce.

Yield: 4 to 6 servings.

Rolled Chicken Breasts

8 boneless, skinless chicken
   breasts
Pepper to taste
4 thin slices boiled ham, halved
4 slices natural Swiss cheese,
   halved
1 (4-ounce) package chipped
   beef
1 (10¾- ounce) can cream of
   mushroom or celery soup
1 (8-ounce) carton sour cream
⅛ cup sherry, optional

Carefully flatten chicken breasts to ¼-inch thickness, using a rolling pin or meat mallet. Sprinkle chicken with pepper and top with slice of ham and cheese. Tuck in sides, roll up and secure with toothpicks. Line an 8 x 12-inch glass baking dish with chipped beef and top with chicken rolls. Combine soup, sour cream and sherry, if desired. Pour over chicken, cover and bake in a preheated 350° oven until tender, about 1½ hours.

Yield: 8 servings.

Spicy Chicken and Rice

3   cups quick rice
1   can diced tomatoes
1   small jar mushrooms, drained
4   ounces light sour cream
½   cup half and half
1   package mushroom soup mix
1   tablespoon freshly ground
    pepper
Salt to taste
2   tablespoons olive oil
¼   cup Dijon mustard
1   can chicken broth
6   boneless chicken breasts

Combine rice, tomatoes and mushrooms and mix well. Add half and half and sour cream and blend thoroughly. Stir in remaining ingredients except chicken breasts and place in a casserole dish or clay cooker. Top with chicken, cover with foil and bake in a preheated 375° oven 30 minutes. Remove foil and continue baking 30 more minutes.

Yield: 6 servings.

"The table is a meeting place, a gathering ground, the source of sustenance and nourishment, festivity, safety, and satisfaction."
—**Laurie Colwin**

Fried Rice with Chicken

2   tablespoons peanut oil
⅓   cup thinly sliced green
    onions
½   teaspoon peeled and minced
    fresh ginger
½   teaspoon minced garlic
2   eggs, lightly beaten
¼   teaspoon salt
¼   teaspoon sugar
2   cooked, boneless chicken
    breasts, cut in pieces
½   cup frozen tiny peas
2   tablespoons soy sauce
2   cups cold cooked rice
½   teaspoon sesame oil

Heat peanut oil in a wok to 325°. Add green onions, ginger and garlic and stir fry 1 minute. Add eggs and scramble lightly, breaking egg up with spatula. Add salt, sugar, chicken, peas and soy sauce and stir fry 2 more minutes. Add cold rice and stir fry 30 seconds. Add sesame oil, stir to combine and serve immediately.

Yield: 4 servings.

Note: This recipe doubles easily and freezes well.

Variation: For Pork Fried Rice, substitute ⅓ pound finely diced ham for chicken.

Chicken and Rice

1½ cups instant rice
1   can cream of celery soup
1   can cream of mushroom
     soup
¾   cup white cooking wine
4   chicken breasts
1   envelope onion soup mix

Place rice in a casserole dish which has been coated with nonstick spray. Mix soups together and pour over rice. Pour wine over soup. Place chicken breasts over rice mixture and sprinkle with soup mix. Seal tightly with foil and bake in a preheated 350° oven for 2 hours.

Yield: 4 servings.

If using boneless chicken breasts, reduce cooking time by 45 minutes.

Sour Cream Enchiladas

1   dozen small tortillas
1   cup vegetable oil
½   cup chopped onion
2   cups grated Cheddar cheese
1   cup cottage cheese
2   cans cream of chicken soup
2   cups boned, cooked chicken
     pieces
½   cup sour cream
1   small can diced green chilies
½   teaspoon salt

Dip tortillas in hot oil to soften. Combine onion and cheeses and divide among tortillas. Roll up and secure with toothpicks. Combine remaining ingredients. Spoon a layer of this mixture into bottom of a casserole dish. Top with tortillas and cover with remaining sauce. Bake in a preheated 350° oven until hot and bubbly, about 30 minutes.

Yield: 6 servings.

"Learn the craft of knowing how to open your heart and to turn on your creativity. There's a light inside of you."

—*Judith Jamison*

Oven Barbecued Chicken

2	chickens, cut into serving pieces
6	tablespoons ketchup
4	tablespoons vinegar
2	tablespoons lemon juice
4	tablespoons Worcestershire sauce
½	cup water
4	tablespoons butter
6	tablespoons brown sugar
2	teaspoons salt
2	teaspoons prepared mustard
2	teaspoons chili powder

Preheat oven to 500°. Place chicken skin-side up in a baking dish. Combine remaining ingredients and pour over chicken. Cook 15 minutes at 500°, then reduce temperature to 350° and continue baking 1 hour more, basting occasionally.

Barbecue Sauce

1	cup chopped onion
½	cup vegetable oil
1	(16-ounce) can tomato sauce
1	cup water
½	cup lemon juice
6	tablespoons Worcestershire sauce
¼	cup prepared mustard
1	teaspoon salt
½	teaspoon pepper
1	bottle barbecue sauce
1	pound brown sugar

Sauté onions in oil in a large saucepan until tender. Add remaining ingredients except brown sugar. Bring to a boil, reduce heat and simmer, uncovered, 15 minutes. Stir in brown sugar.

Delicious on pork chops, ribs and chicken. Keeps indefinitely in refrigerator.

A Simple Pleasure...

Getting up very early in the morning to start on a road trip before anyone's up, watching the sky grow rosy before sunrise, smelling the dewy fields out the car window.

Hot Chicken Supreme

3 cooked, diced chicken breasts
1½ cups chopped celery
1 cup shredded sharp Cheddar cheese
1 cup mayonnaise
¼ cup milk
¼ cup slivered almonds
¼ cup chopped pimento, optional
2 teaspoons chopped onion
½ teaspoon poultry seasoning
½ teaspoon grated lemon rind
1 (3-ounce) can Chinese noodles

Combine all ingredients except noodles and spoon into a greased 1½-quart casserole dish. Top with noodles and bake in a preheated 350° oven for 30 minutes.

Yield: 6 to 8 servings.

Impossible Chicken and Broccoli Pie

2 (6¾-ounce) cans chunk chicken, well-drained
1 (10-ounce) package frozen chopped broccoli, rinsed and drained
1½ cups shredded sharp cheese
1 cup milk
3 eggs
½ cup biscuit baking mix
¼ teaspoon seasoned salt
¼ teaspoon dried thyme

SAVORY TOPPING:

½ cup biscuit baking mix
¼ cup chopped nuts
¼ cup grated Parmesan cheese
⅛ teaspoon garlic powder
2 tablespoons chilled butter or margarine

Layer chicken, broccoli and cheese in a greased 9-inch pie plate. Place remaining ingredients in blender and process on high 15 seconds. Pour over chicken.

For Topping: Combine all ingredients except butter in a small bowl. Cut in butter to form coarse crumbs. Sprinkle over pie and bake in a preheated 400° oven until a knife inserted in center comes out clean, 15 to 20 minutes. Cool 5 minutes before cutting.

Yield: 4 to 6 servings.

Easy Chicken and Broccoli Casserole

1   package frozen broccoli
3   (5-ounce) cans white
    premium chicken, drained
2   cans low-fat cream of
    chicken soup
½   cup milk
½   cup mayonnaise
3   tablespoons lemon juice
1   teaspoon cayenne pepper
1   (8-ounce) container chicken
    flavored stuffing mix

Cook broccoli in a glass baking dish in microwave according to package directions. Top with chicken. Combine soup, milk, mayonnaise, lemon juice and cayenne in a mixing bowl. Pour over chicken. Top with stuffing mix and bake in a preheated 350° oven for 20 to 30 minutes.

Yield: 12 servings.

Ginney's Chicken and Dumplings

1   whole chicken or 6 breasts
1   onion, sliced
1   cube chicken bouillon
Chopped parsley to taste
Pepper to taste
½   cup butter
3-5 cups self-rising flour
½   cup milk

Place chicken, onion, bouillon, parsley and pepper in a large stock pot. Cover with water, bring to a boil, reduce heat to medium and cook until tender. Remove chicken, cool and debone. Remove and discard onion and parsley. There should be enough broth to half-fill stock pot. If not, add canned chicken broth. Bring broth to a boil and add butter. Mix flour with enough water to form a stiff dough. Drop by small teaspoons into a rolling boil. Stir frequently. Reduce heat and simmer, covered, for 20 minutes, stirring frequently. Add milk and simmer 5 minutes. Add chicken, salt and pepper to taste. Turn off heat and cover until ready to serve.

"Wheresoever you go, go with all your heart."
            —*Confucious*

Grandma's Chicken and Dumplings

1 medium chicken
2 cups all-purpose flour
1 1/4 teaspoons baking powder
3/4 teaspoon salt
1 tablespoon shortening
2/3 cup milk

Place chicken in a stock pot and cover with water. Bring to a boil, reduce heat, cover and cook on medium heat until tender, about 2 hours. Remove from broth, cool and, when cool enough to handle, debone. Remove broth from heat. Combine flour, baking powder and salt in a bowl. Cut in shortening until crumbly. Add milk and mix well. Roll dough out to 1/4-inch thickness. Using a pizza cutter, cut dough into 1" x 2" rectangles. Return broth to a boil. Drop dumplings into broth. Add chicken and stir slightly. Cover very tightly with foil and then add lid. Cook on low heat for 15 minutes.

Yield: 8 servings.

"Make a nest of pleasant thoughts."
—John Ruskin

Chicken and Green Bean Casserole

2 cans French-style green beans, drained
4 cooked boneless chicken breasts, cut in bite-size pieces
2 cans cream of chicken soup
1/2 cup mayonnaise
1 sleeve round buttery crackers, crushed
1/2 cup margarine, melted

Spread green beans in bottom of a buttered 2-quart casserole dish. Top with chicken. Combine soup and mayonnaise in a bowl and spread over chicken. Mix cracker crumbs and margarine and sprinkle over soup mixture. Bake, covered, in a preheated 350° oven until bubbly, 30 to 40 minutes.

Reduce fat by using lower fat soup and mayonnaise and substituting bread crumbs for cracker crumbs.

Poppy Seed Chicken

1	whole chicken, cooked, deboned and chopped
2	cans cream of chicken soup
1	(8-ounce) carton sour cream
1	sleeve round buttery crackers, crushed
3	tablespoons poppy seeds
½	cup margarine, melted

Layer half of chicken in a 9 x 13-inch baking dish. Combine soup and sour cream and spoon half over chicken. Top with half of cracker crumbs and drizzle with half of margarine. Sprinkle with half of poppy seeds. Repeat layers and bake in a preheated 350° oven until bubbly, 20 to 25 minutes.

Yield: 8 to 10 servings.

"I learned early on that setting a table is so much more than just laying down knives and forks. It is creating a setting for food and conversation, setting a mood and an aura that lingers long after what was served and who said what was forgotten."
—Peri Wolfman

Cajun Fried Whole Turkey

1	(12 to 15-pound) turkey
1	pint Cajun injector poultry marinade

Cajun seasoning
Peanut oil

The most moist, delicious turkey ever.

Inject turkey with marinade and rub down with Cajun seasoning. Tie legs together and refrigerate overnight. Add enough peanut oil to cover turkey to a 5-gallon deep fryer and heat to 350°. (This is best done outdoors on a hot plate.) Carefully lower turkey into oil and fry 4 minutes per pound. When done, drain well, carve and serve.

Hint: To prevent turkey from sticking to bottom of fryer, place an inverted aluminum pie plate which has been punctured in several places in the bottom of fryer before filling with oil.

Chicken Breast Stroganoff

6   boneless chicken breasts, cut into small strips
1½ tablespoons butter
1½ cups sliced mushrooms
2   tablespoons chopped parsley
2   teaspoons chopped chives
¼   teaspoon dill
Salt
Pepper
½   cup chicken broth
1   tablespoon flour
1   cup sour cream
Hot cooked noodles or rice

Brown chicken in butter in a large skillet over medium heat. Add mushrooms, parsley, chives, dill, salt and pepper. Cook until mushrooms are tender. Stir in broth and simmer 10 minutes. Combine flour and sour cream in a small bowl. Stir into chicken mixture and cook until just heated, being careful not to let boil. Serve over noodles or rice.

Yield: 4 servings.

Skillet Lasagna

1   pound ground beef
2   tablespoons butter
1   envelope spaghetti sauce
1   (16-ounce) container cottage cheese
8   ounces uncooked lasagna noodles
2   teaspoons basil
1   tablespoon parsley flakes
1   teaspoon salt
1   (1-pound) can tomatoes, chopped
1   (8-ounce) can tomato sauce
1   cup water
8   ounces shredded mozzarella cheese

Brown meat in butter in a 12-inch skillet. Drain and sprinkle with half of sauce mix. Spoon cottage cheese over meat and top with noodles. Sprinkle with remaining sauce mix, basil, parsley and salt. Pour tomatoes, tomato sauce and water over all, making sure all ingredients are moistened. Bring to a boil, reduce heat and simmer 35 minutes. Sprinkle with cheese and let stand until cheese is melted, about 5 minutes.

A Simple Pleasure...

The smell of a new baby doll in my Christmas stocking when I was a child.

Lasagne Louise

I	pound ground beef
½	onion, chopped
I	tablespoon basil leaves
I½	teaspoons salt
I	(I-pound) can tomatoes
2	(6-ounce) cans tomato paste
5	ounces lasagna noodles
2	eggs, lightly beaten
I	carton cottage cheese
½	cup grated Parmesan cheese
2	tablespoons parsley flakes
I	teaspoon salt
½	teaspoon pepper
2	packages sliced mozzarella cheese

Brown meat and drain. Add onion, basil, salt, tomatoes and tomato paste, bring to a boil, reduce heat and simmer, uncovered, for 30 minutes, stirring occasionally. Cook noodles as directed on package and drain. Combine eggs, cottage cheese, Parmesan, parsley, salt and pepper. Layer half of noodles in a 9 x 13-inch baking dish. Spread with half of cottage cheese mixture and top with half of mozzarella cheese and half of meat sauce. Repeat layers. Bake in a preheated 375° oven until bubbly, about 30 minutes. Let stand 10 minutes before serving.

Yield: 8 servings.

Zucchini Lasagna

12	lasagna noodles
I	(32-ounce) jar spaghetti sauce with mushrooms
24-30	ounces cottage cheese
3	large zucchini, sliced
24	ounces shredded mozzarella cheese

Dried basil
Dried parsley
Grated Parmesan cheese

Cook lasagna noodles according to package directions and drain. Spread some of sauce in a buttered 9 x 13-inch baking pan. Top with a third of noodles, a third of cottage cheese, a third of zucchini and a third of mozzarella, sprinkling each layer with basil and parsley. Repeat until all ingredients are used. Sprinkle with extra mozzarella and Parmesan cheese. Cover with foil and bake in a preheated 375° oven 30 minutes. Remove foil and continue cooking until bubbly, about 15 more minutes.

"The best thing about the future is that it only comes one day at a time."
—Abraham Lincoln

Chicken Spaghetti

4   large skinless chicken breasts, cooked, deboned and shredded, with cooking broth reserved
1   large package vermicelli or angel hair pasta
8   ounces pasteurized process cheese, cubed
1   large can tiny green peas

Cook pasta according to package directions, using reserved broth. Drain, leaving a small amount of broth in pan. Melt cheese in broth on low heat. Add peas, noodles, chicken and additional water. Mix thoroughly and serve.

Yield 8 servings.

"There is a big difference between living and just breathing. Choose to live, not just exist. Use your gifts and your days wisely, deliberately. You were put here for a purpose."
—**Paul C. Brownlow**

Baked Spaghetti

1   cup chopped onion
1   cup chopped green bell pepper
1   tablespoon margarine or butter
1   (28-ounce) can chopped tomatoes with juice
1   can sliced ripe olives, drained
1   can mushrooms, drained
2   teaspoons oregano
2   pounds ground chuck, cooked and drained
2   cups shredded Cheddar cheese
1   (10¾-ounce) can cream of mushroom soup
¼   cup water
¼   cup grated Parmesan cheese
12 ounces thin spaghetti, broken, cooked and drained

Sauté onion and green pepper in butter in a large skillet. Add tomatoes, mushrooms, olives, oregano and ground beef. Bring to a boil, reduce heat and simmer, uncovered, for 10 minutes. Place half of spaghetti in a greased 9 x 13-inch baking dish. Top with half of tomato mixture and sprinkle with half of Cheddar cheese. Repeat layers. Mix soup and water until smooth. Pour over casserole and sprinkle with Parmesan cheese. Bake, uncovered, in a preheated 350° oven for 30 to 35 minutes.

Yield: 12 servings.

Dressed Chicken Breasts with Angel Hair Pasta

1 cup prepared Ranch salad dressing
⅓ cup Dijon mustard
6 chicken breasts, skinned, boned and pounded thin
½ cup butter
⅓ cup dry white wine
10 ounces angel hair pasta, cooked and drained
Chopped parsley

Whisk salad dressing and mustard together in a small bowl. Sauté chicken in butter in a medium skillet until brown. Transfer to a dish and keep warm. Pour wine into skillet and cook 5 minutes, scraping up any browned bits from skillet. Whisk in dressing mixture, blending well. Spoon sauce over chicken and pasta and garnish with parsley.

Yield: 6 servings.

"When we are authentic, when we keep our spaces simple, simply beautiful living takes place."
—Alexandra Stoddard

Cheesy Chicken and Shrimp Spaghetti

1½ pounds chicken, cooked and deboned, with cooking broth reserved
1 pound vermicelli
1 medium onion, chopped
1 tablespoon margarine
1 pound pasteurized process cheese, cubed
1 can mushrooms, drained
1 can cream of mushroom soup
1 can cream of chicken soup
1 can tomatoes and green chilies, partially drained
1 pound medium shrimp, cooked and peeled

Cook noodles according to package directions, using reserved broth. Drain. Brown onion in margarine. Add cheese, mushrooms, soups and tomatoes. Heat just until cheese melts. Add noodles, chicken and half of shrimp. Place in a 9 x 13-inch baking dish and top with remaining shrimp. Bake in a preheated 350° oven for 30 minutes.

Yield: 12 to 14 servings.

MeMe's Spaghetti

1 (12-ounce) package thin spaghetti, broken
1½ pounds ground beef
1 pound hot sausage
1 large onion, chopped
1 (1-pound) can tomatoes, chopped
1 (10-ounce) can tomatoes and green chilies, optional
1 package spaghetti sauce mix
1 pound grated Cheddar cheese

Cook spaghetti according to package directions and drain. Brown ground beef, sausage and onions and drain well. Add tomatoes, tomatoes and chilies and sauce mix. Bring to a boil, reduce heat and simmer 10 minutes. Place spaghetti in a 9 x 13-inch baking pan and top with sauce and cheese. Mix well, cover and bake in a preheated 350° oven for 30 to 45 minutes.

Yield: 6 to 8 servings.

Beef with Tomatoes and Green Chilies

2 pounds ground beef
1 green bell pepper, finely chopped
1 large onion, finely chopped
¾ cup margarine
7 ounces angel hair pasta
2 beef bouillon cubes
1 can tomatoes and green chilies
1 can English peas, drained
2 tablespoons Worcestershire sauce
6 ounces shredded cheese, divided

Brown ground beef and drain. Sauté onion and bell pepper in butter. Cook pasta in water with bouillon cubes. Drain, reserving a third of the water. Add tomatoes and green chilies, onions and pepper and Worcestershire sauce. Stir in peas, 2 ounces of cheese, beef and pasta. Place half of mixture in an 9 x 11-inch pan and sprinkle with 2 ounces cheese. Top with remaining mixture and remaining cheese. Bake in a preheated 350° oven for 1 hour.

"The art of being happy is the art of discovering the depths that lie in the common daily things."
—Brierley

Miss Daisy's Beef Casserole

2 pounds lean ground beef
1 cup diced celery
¼ cup diced green bell pepper
¾ cup chopped onion
1 (29-ounce) can tomatoes
1 (16-ounce) can tomatoes
1 (8-ounce) can mushroom pieces, drained
1 (8-ounce) can sliced water chestnuts, drained
1 cup cubed American process cheese
½ cup chopped green olives
½ cup chopped black olives
½ teaspoon salt
¼ teaspoon pepper
1 (6-ounce) package egg noodles, uncooked
2 cups shredded Cheddar cheese

Brown beef and drain. Add celery, green pepper and onion and sauté until tender. Add tomatoes and their juice. Add remaining ingredients, except for Cheddar cheese. Bring to a boil, reduce heat and simmer for 20 minutes. Pour into a 9 x 13-inch casserole and top with Cheddar cheese. Bake, uncovered, in a preheated 350° oven for 30 minutes.

Yield: 8 servings.

Great for pot luck suppers.

HORSERADISH SAUCE

1 cup sour cream
1 tablespoon horseradish sauce
1 teaspoon white vinegar
¼ teaspoon sugar
Dash of hot pepper sauce
Dash of salt

Combine all ingredients and chill.

Good with baked ham and prime rib.

Marzetti

1½ pounds ground chuck
1 medium green bell pepper, chopped
1 medium onion, finely chopped
1 tablespoon chili powder
1 teaspoon garlic salt
1 can cream of mushroom soup
1 can tomato soup
½ cup water
½ cup hot taco sauce
8 ounces fine or medium egg noodles
½ cup grated Cheddar cheese
½ cup shredded mozzarella cheese

Cook beef, green pepper and onion until beef is brown and vegetables are tender. Drain well. Add chili powder, garlic salt, soups, water and taco sauce. Bring to a boil, reduce heat and simmer 10 to 15 minutes, stirring occasionally. Cook noodles according to package directions and drain. Place in a large glass baking dish and top with beef mixture. Sprinkle with cheeses. The heat of the beef mixture should melt the cheese. If not, heat in microwave until cheese melts.

Yield: 6 to 8 servings.

Sausage Rigatoni with Sun-Dried Tomatoes

1 pound Italian sausage, sliced
1 (28-ounce) can crushed tomatoes
1½ ounces dry sun-dried tomatoes
2 tablespoons fresh basil
1 teaspoon fresh thyme
2 cloves garlic, minced
¾ cup water
8 ounces rigatoni pasta

Brown sausage over medium heat in a large saucepan. Drain and add remaining ingredients except pasta. Bring to a boil, reduce heat and simmer 15 minutes. Meanwhile, cook pasta according to package directions and drain. Serve sauce over pasta.

Yield: 4 servings.

Note: Dried herbs may be used if fresh are unavailable; reduce amount used by two-thirds.

"A small house will hold as much happiness as a big one."
—Anonymous

Roasted Vegetables and Linguine

8   Roma tomatoes, chopped
1   unpeeled eggplant, cut up
1   red bell pepper, cut up
1   zucchini, sliced
4   cloves garlic, minced
3   tablespoons olive oil, divided
3   tablespoons fresh basil
½   teaspoon salt
¼   teaspoon pepper
8   ounces linguine
½   cup shredded fresh Parmesan cheese

Good way to use fresh vegetables and herbs.

Preheat oven to 450°. Place tomatoes, eggplant, bell pepper, zucchini and garlic in a large bowl. Toss with 2 tablespoons olive oil, basil, salt and pepper. Place in a 10 x 15-inch baking pan which has been coated with nonstick spray. Bake until vegetables are tender and slightly brown, about 15 minutes. Cook linguine according to package directions and drain. Place in a serving bowl, add remaining olive oil and the vegetables. Toss to mix and sprinkle with Parmesan.

Yield: 6 servings.

Fettuccine Alfredo

10   ounces fettuccine
2   tablespoons butter

SAUCE:

¾   cup butter or margarine
1   cup half and half
1½   cups grated Parmesan cheese
3   tablespoons minced dried onion
3-4 tablespoons minced chives
2   tablespoons fresh chopped parsley
1   cup sour cream
Dash of garlic salt

Cook pasta according to package directions and drain. Toss with butter and keep hot.

For Sauce: Melt butter in a saucepan over low heat. Add cream and cheese and stir until cheese is melted. Add remaining ingredients and cook, stirring, over low heat, until heated through. Do not boil. Pour over noodles, toss and serve.

Yield: 10 servings.

Desserts

Cheese Cake

4   (8-ounce) packages cream
      cheese, softened
1½ cups sugar
4   eggs
1   teaspoon lemon juice
1   tablespoon vanilla
2   tablespoons flour
2   tablespoons cornstarch
½ cup butter
1   pint sour cream

Beat cream cheese and sugar in a mixing bowl until light and fluffy. Add eggs one at a time, beating well after each addition. Mix in vanilla, lemon juice, flour and cornstarch by hand. Melt butter and add to cheese mixture. Mix again and fold in sour cream. Pour into a 9-inch spring-form pan and bake in a preheated 325° oven for 1 hour. Turn off oven and leave cake in oven for 2 hours. Remove and chill. Serve with fruit topping.

Yield: 12 servings.

Chocolate Pound Cake

1   cup margarine, softened
3   cups sugar
½ cup vegetable oil
5   eggs
3   cups all-purpose flour
¼ teaspoon salt
½ teaspoon baking powder
½ cup cocoa
1½ cups milk
1   teaspoon vanilla

CHOCOLATE ICING:

3   cups sugar
3   tablespoons cocoa
1   (8¼-ounce) can evaporated
      milk
1½ teaspoons vanilla
¾ cup margarine, softened

Beat margarine, sugar and oil until smooth. Add eggs one at a time, beating well after each addition. Combine flour, salt, baking powder and cocoa. Add to creamed mixture alternately with milk. Add vanilla and pour into a tube pan which has been coated with nonstick spray. Bake in a preheated 325° oven until a tester inserted in center comes out clean, about 1½ hours. Cool.

For Icing: Place sugar, cocoa and milk in a saucepan and bring to a rolling boil. Cook 4½ minutes, stirring constantly. Remove from heat. Blend margarine and vanilla in a mixing bowl. Add cooked mixture and beat until mixture becomes grainy. Cool overnight in refrigerator and ice cake the following day.

Italian Cream Cake

½ cup shortening
½ cup margarine, softened
2 cups sugar
5 eggs, separated
2 cups all-purpose flour
1 teaspoon baking soda
1 cup buttermilk
1 teaspoon vanilla
1 (7-ounce) can flaked coconut
1 cup chopped pecans

CREAM FROSTING:

1 (8-ounce) package cream
   cheese, softened
¼ cup margarine, softened
1 box confectioners sugar
1 teaspoon vanilla
½ cup chopped pecans

Cream shortening and margarine. Add sugar and beat until smooth. Add eggs yolks and beat well. Combine flour and soda and add to creamed mixture alternately with buttermilk. Stir in vanilla, coconut and nuts. Beat egg whites in another bowl with clean beaters until stiff. Fold into batter and pour batter into 3 greased and floured 9-inch cake pans. Bake in a preheated 350° oven until a tester inserted in center comes out clean, about 25 minutes. Cool and frost.

For Cream Frosting: Beat cream cheese and margarine until light and fluffy. Add sugar and mix well. Add vanilla and nuts and beat until smooth. Spread over cooled cake.

Fresh Apple Cake

3 eggs, lightly beaten
2 cups sugar
1¼ cups vegetable oil
2½ cups self-rising flour
2½ medium apples, chopped
1 cup raisins
1 cup coconut
1 cup chopped pecans

TOPPING:

¼ cup butter
½ cup firmly packed brown
   sugar
⅓ cup milk

Blend eggs, oil and sugar with a mixer until creamy. Add flour a little at a time and blend well. Batter will be stiff. Fold in remaining ingredients and pour into a greased and floured tube pan. Bake in a preheated 350° oven until a tester inserted in center comes out clean, about 1 hour. Cool in pan 30 minutes before inverting on serving plate.

For Topping: Combine all ingredients in a small saucepan and boil for 3 minutes. Pour over cake.

Carrot Cake

2   cups sugar
1   cup oil
5   eggs
2   cups flour
1   teaspoon cinnamon
2   teaspoons baking powder
2   teaspoons baking soda
3   cups grated carrots
1   cup chopped walnuts

FROSTING:

1   (8-ounce) package cream cheese, softened
½   cup butter, softened
1   box confectioners sugar
1   teaspoon vanilla

Mix sugar and oil in a large bowl. Beat in eggs one at a time. Sift in flour, baking powder, soda and cinnamon. Mix in carrots and nuts and pour into 3 greased and lightly floured 9-inch cake pans. Bake in a preheated 350° oven until a tester inserted in center comes out clean, about 30 minutes. Cool.

For Frosting: Beat cream cheese, butter and sugar until light and fluffy. Stir in vanilla and spread on cooled cake.

Cream Cheese Pound Cake

1   cup margarine, softened
½   cup butter, softened
1   (8-ounce) package cream cheese, softened
6   eggs
3   cups sugar
3   cups all-purpose flour
2   teaspoons vanilla

Cream together butter, margarine and cream cheese. Add eggs one at a time, beating well after each addition. Slowly add sugar and flour and blend well. Add vanilla. Pour into a greased and floured tube pan. Place in a COLD oven. DO NOT PRE-HEAT. Turn oven to 300° and bake 1½ hours.

"A little of what you fancy does you good."
—*Marie Lloyd*

Toffee Candy Bar Cake Delight

1 (2-layer) package German chocolate cake mix
1 (14-ounce) can sweetened condensed milk
1 (16-ounce) jar caramel ice cream topping
8 ounces light whipped topping
3 toffee candy bars, crushed

Prepare cake using package directions. Bake in a 9 x 13-inch pan in a preheated 350° oven. Pierce entire surface of hot cake with a fork and pour condensed milk over cake. Spread with caramel topping. Cover and refrigerate for 3 to 4 hours. Spread with whipped topping and sprinkle with crushed candy. Store in refrigerator.

A Simple Pleasure...
Eating the golden crusty skin of a roasted marshmallow done to perfection over hot coals.

Strawberry Cake

1 package yellow cake mix
2 pints fresh strawberries
1 package strawberry glaze
1 (8-ounce) package cream cheese, softened
½ cup confectioners sugar
½ cup sugar
1 (12-ounce) container frozen whipped topping, thawed

Bake cake according to package directions and cool. Slice each layer in half horizontally. Slice strawberries and cover with glaze. Combine cream cheese and sugars and beat until light and fluffy. Fold in whipped topping. Spread a quarter of mixture over cooled cake layer and top with a quarter of strawberries. Place second cake layer over strawberries and repeat layering. Do not frost sides of cake.

Hundred Dollar Cake

5   eggs, separated
3   cups sifted all-purpose flour
4   teaspoons cocoa
¼   teaspoon salt
1   teaspoon baking soda
2½ cups sugar
1   cup shortening
1   cup buttermilk
5   tablespoons perked coffee
2   teaspoons vanilla

ICING:

¾   cup margarine, softened
1½ boxes confectioners sugar
1   tablespoon cocoa
4   tablespoons perked coffee
1½ teaspoons vanilla

Beat egg whites until stiff and set aside. Sift together flour, cocoa, salt and baking soda. Cream shortening and sugar until light and fluffy. Add egg yolks and blend. Add dry ingredients alternately with buttermilk. Stir in coffee and vanilla and fold in egg whites. Pour into 3 greased and floured cake pans and bake in a preheated 350° oven until a tester inserted in center comes out clean, 35 to 40 minutes. Cool completely before icing.

For Icing: Beat margarine until fluffy. Gradually beat in sugar until well-blended. Stir in cocoa, coffee and vanilla.

Lemon Poppy Seed Sour Cream Sheet Cake

¼   cup butter or margarine
½   cup milk
1   egg, lightly beaten
8   ounces sour cream
2   packages lemon poppy seed muffin mix

LEMON GLAZE:

1   cup sifted confectioners sugar
2   teaspoons lemon juice
2   teaspoons water

Melt butter in a saucepan over low heat. Remove from heat and stir in remaining ingredients in order listed. Spread in a greased 9 x 13-inch baking pan and bake in a preheated 350° oven until golden brown, 25 to 28 minutes. Cool in pan about 2 minutes and spread with glaze.

For Glaze: Combine all ingredients and stir until smooth.

Applesauce Cake

½ cup butter, softened
1 cup sugar
2 eggs, lightly beaten
2 cups all-purpose flour, sifted
½ teaspoon baking soda
1 cup unsweetened applesauce
½ teaspoon nutmeg
1 teaspoon cinnamon
½ teaspoon allspice
½ cup chopped pecans
1 cup raisins

Cream together butter and sugar. Add eggs and mix well. Sift together flour and soda and add to creamed mixture alternately with applesauce. Add spices and beat well. Stir in nuts and raisins and pour into a greased and floured Bundt pan. Bake in a preheated 350° oven until a tester inserted in center comes out clean, about 1 hour.

Especially good on cool fall days with a cup of hot tea.

Black Walnut Pound Cake

1 cup butter, softened
½ cup shortening
3 cups sugar
5 eggs
3 cups all-purpose flour
½ teaspoon baking powder
1 cup milk
½ teaspoon vanilla
1 cup coarsely chopped black walnuts

Cream butter and shortening at medium speed with an electric mixture until light and fluffy, about 2 minutes. Gradually add sugar, beating at medium speed 5 to 7 minutes. Add eggs one at a time, beating just until yellow disappears. Combine flour and baking powder and add to creamed mixture alternately with milk, beginning and ending with flour mixture. Mix just until blended after each addition. Stir in vanilla and walnuts. Pour into a greased and floured 10-inch tube pan. Bake in a preheated 325° oven until a tester inserted in center comes out clean, about 1½ hours. Cool in pan 10 to 15 minutes, remove from pan and let cool completely on a wire rack.

Baked cake may be stored, frozen, for 3 to 5 months. Thaw and, if desired, reheat to serve.

Myra Hammond's Prune Cake

2 cups sifted cake flour
1¼ teaspoons baking soda
2½ teaspoons baking powder
½ teaspoon salt
1 teaspoon cinnamon
1 teaspoon nutmeg
1 teaspoon allspice
1½ cups sugar
3 eggs, lightly beaten
1 cup buttermilk
1 cup cooked, mashed prunes
1 cup chopped pecans
¾ cup vegetable oil

GLAZE:

1 cup sugar
1 tablespoon corn syrup
½ cup buttermilk
½ cup butter or margarine
1 teaspoon vanilla

Sift together flour, soda, baking powder, salt and spices. Stir in remaining ingredients and blend well. Pour into a greased and floured 9 x 13-inch baking pan and bake in a preheated 325° oven until a tester inserted in center comes out clean, about 40 minutes. While cake bakes, make glaze.

For Glaze: Combine all ingredients except vanilla in a saucepan. Bring to a boil, and boil, stirring constantly, for 2 minutes. Remove from heat and stir in vanilla. Spread over hot cake.

Jam Cake

2 cups sugar
4 eggs
1 cup blackberry jam
2 cups all-purpose flour
1 teaspoon cinnamon
1 teaspoon allspice
1 teaspoon cloves
1 cup buttermilk
1 teaspoon baking soda
1 cup vegetable oil

CARAMEL FROSTING:

4 cups sugar, divided
1 cup milk
½ cup butter

Cream sugar and eggs. Add jam, flour and spices and mix well. Stir soda into buttermilk, add to batter and mix well. Stir in oil and mix well. Pour into 3 greased and floured 8-inch cake pans and bake in a preheated 325° oven until a tester inserted in center comes out clean, about 25 minutes. Turn onto cooling racks and cool completely.

For Frosting: Caramelize 1 cup sugar. Combine remaining sugar with milk and butter in a large saucepan and cook until a soft ball forms in cold water. Stir in caramelized sugar and beat until of a spreading consistency. Spread over cooled cake.

Apple Date Dream Cake Squares

2 cups all-purpose flour
1 cup sugar
1½ teaspoons baking soda
1 teaspoon salt
1 teaspoon cinnamon
½ teaspoon allspice
2 eggs, lightly beaten
1 (21-ounce) can apple pie
   filling
½ cup vegetable oil
1 teaspoon vanilla
1 cup chopped dates
¼ cup chopped walnuts
Sweetened whipped cream,
   optional
Walnut halves, optional

Combine flour, sugar, soda, salt, cinnamon and allspice in a bowl. Stir gently. In a separate bowl, combine eggs, pie filling, oil and vanilla. Stir into dry ingredients. Stir in dates and walnuts and pour into a greased and floured 9 x 13-inch baking pan. Bake in a preheated 350° oven until a tester inserted in center comes out clean, 35 to 40 minutes. Cool and cut into squares. Top each square with whipped cream and an walnut half before serving, if desired.

Pumpkin Roll

¾ cup all-purpose flour
1 teaspoon baking powder
3 eggs
1 cup sugar
⅔ cup mashed pumpkin
1 teaspoon lemon juice
1 teaspoon ginger
2 teaspoons cinnamon
½ teaspoon nutmeg
½ teaspoon salt

FILLING:

1 (8-ounce) package cream
   cheese, softened
1 cup confectioners sugar
4 tablespoons margarine,
   softened
1 teaspoon vanilla
1 cup chopped pecans, optional

Mix all roll ingredients together and beat for 2 minutes. Spread in a greased and floured jelly roll pan or cookie sheet. Bake in a preheated 325° oven until a tester inserted in center comes out clean, about 15 minutes. Turn immediately onto a towel which has been sprinkled well with confectioners sugar. Roll up in towel and cool.

For Filling: Combine all ingredients. Unroll cooled roll and spread with filling. Re-roll and sprinkle with confectioners sugar, if desired. Cover and chill.

Pecan Tarts

1   (3-ounce) package cream
    cheese, softened
½   cup butter, softened
1   cup sifted all-purpose flour
1   egg, lightly beaten
¾   cup firmly packed brown
    sugar
1   teaspoon vanilla
⅛   teaspoon salt
⅔   cup chopped pecans

Blend cream cheese and butter. Add flour, blending well. Cover and refrigerate for one hour. Shape into 24 balls and press into small muffin pans, covering sides and bottoms of cups. Beat egg, brown sugar, vanilla and salt together just until smooth. Add nuts and stir well. Divide among muffin cups and bake in a preheated 350° oven for 30 minutes.

May be frozen.

Peanut Butter Cookies

1   cup firmly packed brown
     sugar
1   cup sugar
1   cup margarine, softened
1   cup peanut butter
1   egg
2¼ cups self-rising flour

Combine sugars. Add to margarine and cream very well. Add egg and peanut butter and mix well. Add flour and mix until blended. Roll a teaspoon of dough into a ball and place on a cookie sheet. Press down with a fork to flatter. Turn fork 90° and flatten again to produce a criss-cross pattern. Repeat until all dough is used. Bake in preheated 350° oven until edges just begin to brown.

"Life is made up, not of great sacrifices or duties, but of little things, in which smiles and kindnesses and small obligations win and preserve the heart."
—Humphrey Davy

Elizabeth's Chocolate Chip Cookies

1   cup shortening or ¾ cup
    butter, softened
½   cup sugar
1   cup firmly packed brown
    sugar
1   teaspoon vanilla
2   eggs
2   cups all-purpose flour
1   teaspoon baking soda
1   teaspoon salt
2   cups mini-chocolate chips
1   cup chopped pecans

Cream shortening, sugars and vanilla until light and fluffy. Add eggs and beat well. Combine flour, baking soda and salt. Add half to creamed mixture and beat until blended. Add remainder and beat again. Stir in chocolate chips and nuts. Drop by teaspoonfuls onto a greased cookie sheet and bake in a preheated 375° oven for 10 minutes.

Toffee-Topped Bars

2   cups firmly packed brown
    sugar
2   cups all-purpose flour
½   cup butter, softened
1   teaspoon baking powder
½   teaspoon salt
1   teaspoon vanilla
1   cup milk
1   egg
1   cup semisweet chocolate
    chips
½   cup chopped walnuts
¼   cup unsweetened flaked
    coconut

Combine brown sugar and flour in a large mixing bowl. Using a pastry cutter, cut in butter until mixture resembles coarse crumbs. Remove 1 cup of mixture and set aside. Add baking powder and salt to mixture in bowl. Lightly beat in vanilla, milk and egg with a fork. Continue beating until a smooth batter forms. Pour batter into a lightly greased 9 x 13-inch baking pan. Combine chocolate chips and walnuts in a small bowl. Fold in coconut. Sprinkle reserved sugar mixture over batter and top with chip mixture. Using a long, flat spatula, spread topping evenly over batter. Bake in a preheated 350° oven for 35 minutes. Transfer pan to a wire rack and cool completely before slicing. Cut into 24 bars with a serrated knife. Store in an airtight container for up to 5 days.

Yield: 24 bars.

Butterscotch Pinwheels

1 cup semisweet chocolate
chips
2 tablespoons shortening
1 (15-ounce) can sweetened
condensed milk
1 cup all-purpose flour
1 teaspoon vanilla

BUTTERSCOTCH
FILLING:

1 cup butterscotch chips
2 tablespoons shortening
½ cup chopped nuts

Melt chocolate chips and shortening over low heat in a large saucepan, stirring constantly. Remove from heat and add milk, flour and vanilla. Blend well. Line a greased jelly roll pan with waxed paper. Grease paper and spread with batter. Bake in a preheated 325° oven for 6 minutes. Turn onto a towel that has been dusted with confectioners sugar. Quickly spread with filling and sprinkle with nuts. Roll up in towel, starting with long side. Wrap and refrigerate. Cut into ¼-inch slices.

For Filling: Melt butterscotch chips and shortening over low heat in a small saucepan, stirring constantly.

Variation: Substitute chocolate mint pieces or peanut butter pieces for the butterscotch.

Yield: 5 dozen.

Butter Squares

1 box chocolate or yellow
butter cake mix
1 egg
½ cup margarine, softened
1 cup chopped nuts, optional
1 box confectioners sugar
1 (8-ounce) package cream
cheese, softened
2 eggs

Combine cake mix, egg and margarine until crumbly and press into bottom of a well-greased 9 x 11-inch pan. Sprinkle with chopped nuts, if desired. Mix remaining ingredients and spread over crumb mixture. Bake in a preheated 350° oven until golden brown, about 35 minutes. Cool and cut into small squares, as they are very rich.

Yield: 10 to 12 servings.

Aunt Louise's Tea Cakes

1¾ cups sugar
1   cup shortening
2   eggs
3   cups self-rising flour
2   teaspoons vanilla or lemon
    flavoring

Preheat oven to 325° 8 to 10 minutes before baking cookies. Cream together sugar and shortening. Add eggs and blend. Gradually mix in flour and flavoring by hand. Place cookies on an ungreased cookie sheet and bake until slightly brown around edges. Do not overbake. Sprinkle with sugar after baking.

Yield: 4 dozen.

Fruit Cake Cookies

½   cup butter, softened
½   cup firmly packed brown
    sugar
3   eggs, separated
2   cups all-purpose flour
½   teaspoon baking soda
½   teaspoon cinnamon
½   teaspoon cloves
½   teaspoon allspice
Dash of salt
½   cup evaporated milk
1½ teaspoons vinegar
2   cups raisins, soaked in water
    overnight
1   pound candied pineapple,
    chopped
1   pound candied cherries,
    halved
1   pound nuts, chopped
2   cups dates, chopped

Cream butter and sugar. Add beaten egg yolks. Combine flour, soda and spices. Mix together milk and vinegar and add to creamed mixture alternately with flour mixture. Add fruits and mix well. Stiffly beat egg whites in a separate bowl with clean beaters. Fold into batter. Drop by teaspoonfuls onto a greased cookie sheet and bake in a preheated 250° oven until lightly golden brown, about 30 minutes.

Molasses Cookies

1   cup sugar
½   cup lard or shortening
1   teaspoon baking soda
½   cup light molasses
1   teaspoon cinnamon
Pinch of salt
½   teaspoon cloves
½   cup boiling water
3½ cups all-purpose flour

Place all ingredients except boiling water and flour in a large bowl. Pour water into bowl and blend. Stir in flour, cover and refrigerate overnight. Roll dough out on a lightly floured surface to ⅛-inch thickness. Cut cookies into desired shapes and place on lightly greased cookie sheets. Bake in a preheated 350° oven for about 12 minutes.

Note: Makes a great gingerbread boy.

Oatmeal Cookies

1   cup shortening
1½ cups sugar
½   cup firmly packed brown
    sugar
2   eggs
½   teaspoon vanilla
1⅓ cups all-purpose flour
1   teaspoon baking soda
¼   teaspoon salt
1   cup chopped pecans
2   cups oats

Combine shortening, sugars, eggs and vanilla in a mixing bowl and beat with mixer on medium-high until light and fluffy, about 4 to 5 minutes. Stir in flour, soda and salt and mix well. Stir in nuts and oats and drop by teaspoonfuls onto an ungreased cookie sheet. Bake in a preheated 325° oven 20 minutes.

Yield: 3 dozen.

"Our life is frittered away by detail. Simplify, simplify."
—Henry David Thoreau

Johnnie Ruth's Coconut Cream Pie

1 cup plus 3 tablespoons sugar, divided
⅓ cup flour
¼ teaspoon salt
2 cups milk
1 tablespoon butter
2 eggs, separated
1 teaspoon vanilla
⅛ teaspoon cream of tartar
1 baked pie crust
1 package frozen coconut

Mix 1 cup sugar, flour and salt in a microwave-safe bowl. Add milk and butter and microwave 2 to 3 minutes. Stir and add beaten egg yolks. Microwave until thickened, 2 to 3 minutes more, stirring once or twice. Add vanilla and pour into pie shell. Beat egg whites with cream of tartar and remaining sugar until stiff. Spread over custard and top with coconut. Brown in oven.

Animal crackers, and cocoa to drink.
That is the finest of suppers, I think;
When I'm grown up and can have what I please
I think I shall always insist upon these.

—Christopher Morley

Johnnie Ruth's Chocolate Pie

1 cup plus 3 tablespoons sugar, divided
⅓ cup flour
¼ cup cocoa
2 cups milk
1 tablespoon butter
2 eggs, separated
1 teaspoon vanilla
⅛ teaspoon cream of tartar
1 baked pie crust

Mix 1 cup sugar, flour and cocoa in a microwave-safe bowl. Add milk and butter and microwave 2 to 3 minutes. Stir and add beaten egg yolks. Microwave until thickened, 2 to 3 minutes more, stirring once or twice. Add vanilla and pour into pie shell. Beat egg whites with cream of tartar and remaining sugar until stiff. Spread over custard. Brown in oven.

German Chocolate Pie

½ cup margarine, softened
4 cups sugar
1 (12-ounce) can evaporated
   milk
6 eggs
⅔ cup cocoa
3 tablespoons flour
Pinch of salt
1 cup chopped pecans
1 (7-ounce) package coconut
1 teaspoon vanilla
3 unbaked 9-inch pie crusts

Cream butter and sugar. Add milk and blend. Add eggs one at a time, blending after each addition. Combine cocoa, flour and salt and add to creamed mixture. Fold in nuts, coconut and vanilla. Pour into pie crusts and bake in a preheated 325° to 350° oven for 35 minutes. Do not overbake. The filling will set up after baking.

'No Roll' Pie Crust

1¼ cups all-purpose flour
½ cup margarine, sliced
½ cup firmly packed light
   brown sugar
⅓ cup coconut or chopped
   nuts

Place all ingredients in a 9-inch pie pan and place in a 400° oven. Stir every 5 minutes until all ingredients are well mixed and brown, about 15 minutes. Remove from oven and press into pan to form a crust. Cool and fill as desired.

Good with butterscotch filling.

It seems to me that our three basic needs, for food and security and love, are so entwined that we connot think of one without the other.
— M.F.K. Fisher

Blueberry Pie

1 cup sugar
¼ cup all-purpose flour
¼ teaspoon salt
½ teaspoon ground cinnamon
4 cups fresh or frozen
   blueberries
1 tablespoon lemon juice
Pastry for 2 crust 9-inch pie,
   unbaked
2 tablespoons butter

Combine all ingredients except crust and butter. Line a 9-inch pie pan with a crust rolled ⅛-inch thick. Turn filling into crust and dot with butter. Cover with remaining pastry, trim edges, turn under and flute. Cut slits in top crust to vent. Bake in a preheated 400° oven for 50 minutes.

Mam's Cobbler Pie

1 carton berries
½ cup butter
½ cup all-purpose flour
1 teaspoon baking powder
½ cup sugar
½ cup milk
2 tablespoons shortening

Place berries in a baking dish. Melt butter and blend with remaining ingredients. Pour batter over fruit and bake in a preheated 400° oven until brown.

"Be happy; let who will be sad, There are so many pleasant things, So many things to make us glad, The flower that buds, the bird that sings, And sweeter still than all of these Are friendship and old memories."

— M.C.D.

Apple Cobbler

½ cup margarine
2 cups sugar
2 cups water
1½ cups sifted self-rising flour
½ cup shortening
⅓ cup milk
2 cups chopped apples
1 teaspoon cinnamon

Melt margarine in a 9 x 13-inch baking dish. Heat sugar and water in a saucepan until sugar dissolves. Place flour in a bowl and cut shortening in until fine crumbs form. Add milk and stir with a fork until dough leaves side of bowl. Turn onto a lightly floured board and knead just until smooth. Roll into a large rectangle ¼-inch thick. Sprinkle apples with cinnamon and arrange apples evenly over dough. Roll up dough jelly roll-style and cut into 16 slices. Place slices in pan with melted margarine. Pour sugar syrup around slices carefully. Bake in a preheated 350° oven for 1 hour.

Yield: 16 servings.

Easy Sweet Potato Pie

2 cups mashed sweet potatoes
1 cup sugar
½ cup margarine, softened
1 teaspoon vanilla
1 baked, cooled pie crust
Whipped cream

Combine potatoes, sugar, margarine and vanilla and stir until well-blended. Pour into pie crust. Top with a dollop of whipped cream before serving.

Yield: 8 servings.

"We blossom under praise like flowers in sun and dew; we open, we reach, we grow."
— Gerhard E. Frost

German Sweet Chocolate Pie

2 egg whites
⅛ teaspoon salt
⅛ teaspoon cream of tartar
½ cup sugar
½ cup finely chopped nuts
½ teaspoon vanilla
4 ounces German sweet chocolate
3 tablespoons water
1 teaspoon vanilla
1 cup whipping cream

Combine egg whites, salt and cream of tartar in a mixing bowl. Beat until foamy. Add sugar, 2 tablespoons at a time, beating after each addition. Continue beating until stiff peaks form. Fold in nuts and vanilla. Spoon into a lightly greased 8-inch pie pan and form a "nest-like" shell by building sides up ½-inch above rim of pan. Bake in a preheated 300° oven 50 to 55 minutes. Place chocolate and water in a saucepan over low heat. Cook, stirring, until chocolate melts. Remove from heat, cool and add vanilla. Whip cream and fold in chocolate mixture. Pile into prepared shell and chill 2 hours before serving.

Blueberry Cream Pie

1 cup sour cream
2 tablespoons all-purpose flour
1 egg, lightly beaten
¾ cups sugar
¼ teaspoon salt
1 teaspoon vanilla
2½ cups fresh blueberries
1 deep-dish 9-inch pie crust, unbaked

TOPPING:

⅓ cup sugar
¾ cup all-purpose flour
6 tablespoons butter, softened

Combine sour cream, flour, egg, sugar, salt and vanilla in a bowl. Beat with an electric mixer until smooth, about 5 minutes. Fold in blueberries and turn into pie crust.

For Topping: Combine sugar and flour in a bowl. Cut in butter until coarse crumbs form. Sprinkle over blueberry mixture and bake in a preheated 400° oven until done, 35 to 40 minutes.

Japanese Fruit Pie

2   cups sugar
1   cup margarine, melted
1   cup coconut
1   cup chopped pecans
2   teaspoons vanilla
4   eggs, beaten
1   cup raisins
2   unbaked pie shells

Combine sugar, margarine, coconut, pecans and vanilla and blend. Add eggs and raisins and pour into pie crusts. Bake in a preheated 300° oven for 50 to 55 minutes. Serve with whipped topping, if desired.

Fresh Peach Pie

1   cup water
1   cup sugar
2   tablespoons flour
1   package peach gelatin
1-1½ cups fresh peach slices
1   baked pie shell
Frozen whipped topping, thawed

Combine water, sugar and flour in a medium saucepan. Bring to a boil and add gelatin. Remove from heat and stir until well-blended. Arrange peaches in pie crust and top with gelatin mixture. Refrigerate for several hours or overnight. Serve with whipped topping.

Yield: 8 servings.

"Happiness is not a station you arrive at, but a manner of traveling."
—Margaret Lee Rumbeck

Grandmother's Apple Pie

3 tart apples, chopped
1 deep-dish pie crust, unbaked
1 cup sugar
¼ cup all-purpose flour
½ teaspoon nutmeg
½ teaspoon cinnamon
¼ cup margarine, melted
½ cup orange juice
1 regular pie crust, unbaked
Vanilla ice cream, optional

Arrange apples in deep-dish crust. Combine sugar, flour, nutmeg and cinnamon. Sprinkle over apples. Pour margarine and orange juice over all. Arrange remaining crust over top and seal. Cut several slits in top to vent and bake in a preheated 350° oven for 1 hour. Serve topped with vanilla ice cream, if desired.

Yield: 8 servings.

"I am beginning to learn that it is the sweet, simple things of life which are the real ones after all."
—Laura Ingalls Wilder

Coconut Caramel Pie

¼ cup margarine
1 (7-ounce) package flaked coconut
½ cup chopped pecans
1 (8-ounce) package cream cheese, softened
1 (14-ounce) can sweetened condensed milk
1 (16-ounce) container frozen whipped topping, thawed
1 (12-ounce) jar caramel ice cream topping
2 (9-inch) pie crusts, baked

Melt margarine in a large skillet. Add coconut and pecans. Cook until golden brown, stirring constantly. Remove from heat. Combine cream cheese and milk, beating with an electric mixer until smooth. Fold in whipped topping. Layer a quarter of mixture into each crust. Drizzle a quarter of caramel sauce over each cream cheese layer and sprinkle with a quarter of coconut mixture. Repeat layers, cover and freeze until firm. Let stand at room temperature 5 minutes before slicing.

Pecan Pie

3   eggs, lightly beaten
⅔   cup sugar
⅓   teaspoon salt
⅓   cup melted butter
1   cup dark corn syrup
1   cup pecan halves
1   (9-inch) pie crust, unbaked

Combine all ingredients except crust and blend. Pour into crust and bake in a preheated 375° oven until center is set and crust is nicely browned, 45 to 50 minutes. Serve cold or slightly warm.

Peanut Butter Pie

1   (8-ounce) package cream cheese, softened
¾   cup confectioners sugar
½   cup creamy peanut butter
2   tablespoons milk
1   (8-ounce) container frozen whipped topping, thawed
1   graham cracker pie crust

Beat cream cheese, sugar, peanut butter and milk until smooth and creamy. Fold in whipped topping and blend. Pour into crust and chill.

Southern Blackberry Cobbler

½   cup butter
2⅓ cups blackberries
1½ cups sugar, divided
1   cup water
1   cup self-rising flour
⅔   cup milk

A prized summer dessert.

Place butter, blackberries, ½ cup sugar and water in an 8-inch square pan and heat until butter melts. Mix flour and remaining sugar in a bowl. Add milk and stir until smooth. Pour evenly over blackberry mixture and bake in a preheated 350° oven for 20 to 25 minutes.

Yield: 10 servings.

Pineapple Chess Pie

2 cups sugar
½ cup margarine, softened
4 eggs
3 tablespoons all-purpose flour
1 (8-ounce) can crushed pineapple, drained
1 teaspoon vanilla
1 (9-inch) pie crust, unbaked

Cream sugar and margarine until light and fluffy. Add eggs and flour and beat well. Stir in pineapple and vanilla and pour into pie crust. Bake in a preheated 350° oven until a knife inserted in center comes out clean, about 45 minutes.

Frozen Lime Torte

1 pint lime sherbet
1 pint lemon sorbet
1 pint frozen vanilla yogurt
1¼ cups graham cracker crumbs
2 tablespoons sugar
¼ cup margarine, melted
1 tablespoon Key Lime juice
¼ cup toasted coconut

Place sherbet, sorbet and yogurt in refrigerator to soften while preparing crust. Combine graham cracker crumbs, sugar and margarine and mix well. Press into bottom of a 9-inch pie pan and freeze 15 minutes. Spoon softened sherbet, sorbet and yogurt into a large bowl. Add lime juice and stir gently. Spoon over crust, spreading evenly. Sprinkle with coconut and press it down lightly. Freeze at least 4 hours, or until firm. To serve, let stand at room temperature for 15 minutes. Cut into wedges.

Yield: 10 servings.

Teach your children how to wash the dishes. The lessons they'll learn are more valuable than the glasses they'll break.
—Parent's Little Book of Wisdom

Cappuccino Meringues with Peppermint Ice Cream and Mocha Drizzle

3   egg whites
½   cup sugar
¾   teaspoon cinnamon
1¼ teaspoons espresso powder
     or instant coffee
¼   teaspoon cream of tartar
⅛   teaspoon salt
1   teaspoon coffee liqueur,
     optional
Unsweetened cocoa powder

MOCHA DRIZZLE:

1   cup butter
2   boxes confectioners sugar
Strongly brewed coffee
Peppermint Ice Cream
Fresh berries
Mint sprigs

Place egg whites in a medium bowl and let stand at room temperature for 30 minutes. Combine sugar, cinnamon and espresso powder in a small bowl. Line 2 baking sheets with foil and coat with nonstick spray. Add cream of tartar and salt to egg whites. Beat with electric mixer on medium speed until soft peaks form. Gradually add sugar mixture, 1 tablespoon at a time, then coffee liqueur, if desired. Beat on high speed until stiff peaks form and sugar is almost dissolved, about 4 to 6 minutes. Drop by rounded teaspoons onto prepared baking sheets and bake in a preheated 300° oven for 25 minutes. Turn off oven and let meringues stand in oven with door closed for 30 minutes. Remove from oven and peel off foil. Cool completely.

For the Mocha Drizzle: Melt butter in a large saucepan and add sugar. Stir in enough coffee to make a creamy consistency.

To Serve: Place a scoop of ice cream in meringue and drizzle with sauce. Garnish with berries and mint sprigs.
Covington's

Ruby Grapefruit and Lemon Granita

4 cups water
2 cups sugar
1 cup fresh lemon juice
1 cup fresh ruby red grapefruit juice
2 tablespoons grated lemon rind
1 tablespoon grated grapefruit rind
2 drops red food coloring

Combine water and sugar in a medium saucepan. Boil for 5 minutes. Remove from heat and cool completely. Add remaining ingredients and pour into a 9 x 13-inch dish. Freeze until nearly hard. Remove from freezer and put into a food processor. Process until smooth and return to pan. Freeze until firm. Remove from freezer 20 minutes before serving.

A beautiful coral-colored dessert.

Yield: 6 to 8 servings.

Lindy's Pecan Pralines

1 teaspoon baking soda
1 cup buttermilk
2 cups sugar
2 tablespoons white corn syrup
1 cup butter or margarine
1 cup chopped pecans

Mix soda and buttermilk in a large heavy saucepan. Stir well and add sugar, syrup and butter. Cook on medium high, stirring constantly, until a medium ball forms in water or it reaches 240° on a candy thermometer. Remove from heat and add nuts. Stir continually until mixture starts to thicken. Quickly drop onto waxed paper by heaping spoonfuls, using one spoon to scoop candy off the other. Cool and store in an airtight container.

Yield: 3 dozen.

"Simple Pleasures are the last refuge of the complex."

—Oscar Wilde

Frozen Strawberries N Cream

1   cup all-purpose flour
½   cup chopped pecans
½   cup butter or margarine,
     melted
¼   cup firmly packed brown
     sugar
1   (10-ounce) package frozen
     strawberries, thawed
1   cup sugar
2   teaspoons fresh lemon juice
2   egg whites
1   cup whipping cream,
     whipped
Sliced fresh strawberries,
     optional

Combine flour, pecans, butter and brown sugar in an 8-inch square baking pan. Stir well and bake in a preheated 350° oven for 20 minutes, stirring occasionally. Cool. Combine strawberries, sugar, lemon juice and egg whites in a large mixing bowl; beat at high speed of electric mixer until stiff peaks form, 10 to 12 minutes. Fold in whipped cream. Press two-thirds of crumb mixture into a 9-inch springform pan. Spoon in strawberry mixture and sprinkle with remaining crumbs. Freeze until firm and serve garnished with fresh strawberries, if desired.

Yield: 8 to 10 servings.

Butterfinger Ice Cream

1   can sweetened condensed
     milk
2   (12-ounce) cans evaporated
     milk
1½   cups sugar
1   teaspoon vanilla
5   Butterfinger candy bars,
     crushed
Milk

Mix condensed milk, evaporated milk, sugar and vanilla and blend well with a mixer. Add candy and pour into an ice cream freezer. Add enough milk to reach the fill line. Freeze according to manufacturer's instructions.

Cherry Delight

2 cups flour
1 cup butter, softened
1 cup chopped pecans
3 cups confectioners sugar
1 (8-ounce) package cream cheese, softened
2 packages whipped topping mix, prepared according to package directions
1 can cherry pie filling

Mix flour, butter and pecans together and spread in bottom of a 9 x 13-inch baking pan. Bake in a preheated 350° oven until golden brown, 15 to 20 minutes. Cool. Beat sugar and cream cheese until light and fluffy. Fold in whipped topping and spread over cooled crust. Refrigerate 1 hour and spread with pie filling.

Apple Crisp

4 cups peeled, sliced apples
1/4 cup water
2 tablespoons plus 1 teaspoon firmly packed brown sugar, divided
2 teaspoons lemon juice
1 teaspoon cinnamon
1/2 cup oats (quick or old-fashioned)
1 tablespoon margarine, softened

Combine apples, water, 4 teaspoons brown sugar, lemon juice and cinnamon and mix well. Arrange in an 8 x 8-inch baking dish which has been coated with nonstick spray. Combine remaining ingredients and sprinkle over apples. Bake in a preheated 375° oven until apples are tender and topping is lightly browned, about 30 minutes.

Yield: 8 servings.

 A Simple Pleasure...
The intimacy of making and sharing food with dear friends at dinner.

Fruit Pizza

CRUST:

½ cup margarine, softened
¾ cup sugar
1 egg
2 cups all-purpose flour
½ teaspoon baking powder
⅛ teaspoon salt
1 teaspoon vanilla

FILLING:

1 (8-ounce) package cream cheese, softened
⅓ cup sugar

FRUITS:

Your choice of apples, bananas, strawberries, kiwi, mandarin oranges, peaches and/or berries

GLAZE:

⅔ cup sugar
2 tablespoons cornstarch
1 cup orange juice
Pinch of salt

Cream margarine and sugar until light and fluffy. Add remaining ingredients and blend well. Press into a pizza pan and bake in a preheated 350° oven for 10 minutes. Combine cream cheese and sugar and spread over cooled crust. Arrange fruit over cream cheese mixture. Boil glaze ingredients together for 1 minute and cool 5 minutes. Pour over fruit.

Yield: 10 servings.

" 'Mid pleasures and palaces though we may roam, be it ever so humble, there's no place like home."
—John Howard Payne

Black Forest Trifle

¼ cup plus 2 tablespoons sugar
¼ cup cocoa
3½ tablespoons cornstarch
2 cups 1% low-fat milk
1 tablespoon margarine
1 (15-ounce) loaf fat-free
   chocolate pound cake
¼ cup cherry flavored liqueur,
   optional
1 (20-ounce) can lite cherry
   pie filling
2 cups reduced calorie frozen
   whipped topping, thawed
Fresh cherries, optional
Chocolate curls, optional

Combine sugar, cocoa and corn-starch in a saucepan. Gradually add milk, stirring with a whisk until smooth. Cook over medium heat, stirring constantly until mixture thickens, 5 to 8 minutes. Remove from heat and add margarine and vanilla, stirring until margarine melts. Cover and chill. Cut cake into 1-inch cubes. Arrange half of cubes in a 3-quart trifle dish; brush with 2 tablespoons liqueur. Spoon half of cherry pie filling over cake and spread half of chocolate mixture over filling. Top with half of whipped topping. Repeat layers with remaining ingredients. Cover and chill at least 8 hours. Garnish with cherries and chocolate curls, if desired.

Yield: 12 servings.

"Now and then it's good to pause in our pursuit of happiness and just be happy."
—**Anonymous**

Chocolate Mousse Loaf

1½ cups chopped walnuts
1   tablespoon water
1   tablespoon white vinegar
¾   cup butter, melted and
      sizzling hot
6   large egg whites
12 ounces semisweet chocolate,
      broken into pieces
3   tablespoons cocoa
⅓   cup sugar
4   large egg yolks

Butter bottom and sides of a 1-quart glass loaf pan. Line bottom with parchment paper and butter the paper. Spread walnuts over bottom and 2 inches up sides of pan, pressing them into place. Reserve remaining nuts. Mix vinegar and water in a small dish. Keep butter hot on the stove. Put egg whites into food processor bowl and begin to process. After 8 seconds, pour vinegar mixture through the feed tube while machine is running. Process until whites are holding their shape, about 1 minute and 45 seconds. With a rubber spatula, gently transfer to a mixing bowl. Pour chocolate, cocoa and sugar into work bowl. Chop chocolate coarsely, then process until chocolate is finely chopped, about 1 minute. With machine running, pour hot butter through the feed tube and process until chocolate is melted, about 1 minute. Stop machine and scrape sides. Add yolks and process 10 seconds. Spoon whites onto chocolate mixture in a ring. Pulse several times to loosen the mixture. Do not overprocess. Using a rubber spatula, transfer to prepared pan. Cover with plastic wrap and refrigerate for 3 hours. Invert onto a serving dish, remove pan and press remaining nuts into mousse. Serve at room temperature.

Crème de Menthe Brownies

1   cup sugar
1   cup sifted all-purpose flour
½   teaspoon salt
½   cup margarine, softened
4   eggs
1   (16-ounce) can chocolate
    syrup
1   teaspoon vanilla
½   cup chopped nuts

FILLING:

½   cup margarine, softened
2   cups sifted confectioners
    sugar
2   tablespoons crème de
    menthe

ICING:

1   (6-ounce) package semisweet
    chocolate chips
6   tablespoons margarine

Combine sugar, flour and salt by hand. Stir in margarine, eggs, syrup and vanilla. Fold in nuts and pour into a greased and floured 9 x 13-inch pan. Bake in a preheated 350° oven for 30 minutes. Cool.

For Filling: Beat margarine and add confectioners sugar. Blend until smooth. Stir in crème de menthe and spread on cooled brownies.

For Icing: Melt chocolate chips and margarine. Cool and spread over filling. Refrigerate 4 hours before serving.

Coffee Tortoni

1   egg white
1   tablespoon instant coffee
    powder
⅛   teaspoon salt
¼   cup plus 2 tablespoons sugar,
    divided
1   cup heavy cream
1   teaspoon vanilla
⅛   teaspoon almond extract
¼   cup finely chopped toasted
    almonds

Combine egg white, coffee powder and salt and beat with an electric mixer until whites are stiff but not dry. Gradually add 2 tablespoons sugar, beating until meringue is stiff and satiny. Whip cream in a separate bowl until stiff. Fold in remaining sugar and flavorings. Fold in meringue and almonds and blend. Pour into 8 (2-ounce) paper cups and freeze until firm.

Yield: 8 servings.

Strawberry Trifle

1   large angel food cake
2   large packages strawberry
     gelatin
2   cups boiling water
2   (10-ounce) packages frozen
     strawberries
1   large plus 1 small package
     vanilla instant pudding
1   large and 1 small container
     frozen whipped topping,
     thawed

Cut cake into thin slices and set aside. Dissolve gelatin in boiling water. Add strawberries and allow to melt. Cool slightly. Mix pudding with cold milk according to package directions and whip until thickened. Place a layer of cake in a trifle dish and saturate with strawberry mixture. Top with a thin layer of pudding and spread with whipped topping. Repeat layering 3 times. For the last layer, top a layer of cake slices with strawberry mixture and let stand a few minutes. Spread with a generous layer of whipped topping, cover and refrigerate at least 4 hours.

Punch Bowl Cake

1   box white cake mix
1   large box vanilla instant
     pudding mix
1   large can strawberry pie
     filling
1   large can crushed pineapple,
     drained
1   large bag frozen coconut
1   cup chopped pecans
1   large container frozen
     whipped topping, thawed

Prepare cake and pudding according to package directions. Slice and crumble cooled cake. Place half of cake in bottom of a punch bowl. Top with half of remaining ingredients in order given. Repeat layering, cover and refrigerate overnight.

Children's Parties

Tea Time Birthday Party

INVITATION:

Sample Wording:
Anna Catherine is celebrating her 4th
Dress up in your party best...
all trimmed with bows and lace,
Hats will be provided at the party place.
Tea time is _____
Bring your favorite bear or doll
We will be waiting to greet you all!

MENU:

Birthday cake shaped like a teapot with cupcakes shaped like teacups

Cookies decorated to look like wide-brimmed straw hats.

Pretzel Wands — pretzel sticks dipped in white chocolate and sprinkled with pink decorating sugar.

Peanut butter and jelly sandwiches shaped like teapots.*

Pink Lemonade

Peanut Butter and Jelly "Teapot" Sandwiches
16 slices bread
1/4 cup creamy peanut butter
2 tablespoons apple jelly
Dash of ground nutmeg

Cut each slice of bread with a teapot-shaped cookie cutter. Combine peanut butter, jelly and nutmeg; spread on half of bread slices and top with remaining slices.

Yield: 8 sandwiches.

DECORATIONS:

Cover table with fancy lace tablecloth. Set a place for each "lady" using grown-up-sized plates and teacups. Set several small nosegays of pink flowers on table for centerpieces. Set up a separate table with small play china for dolls.

PARTY FAVORS:

Lacy gloves

Long pearl necklaces

Wide-brimmed straw hats decorated with ribbons and tulle and silk flowers

A Children's Luau

INVITATIONS:

Find a Luau theme invitation and write or have
printed your party details. Include a message such as:
A Luau is in the making.
Come along and let's start shaking!
Grass skirts, straw hats, flowers and leis,
Are waiting for you, so don't delay!
ALOHA!

For older children, write the invitation on a slip of paper and place it in a washed
clam shell tied with raffia strips. Hand deliver or place in a small box to mail.

MENU

Pineapple, Cheese and Cherry Skewers Served in Fresh Pineapple*
Fresh Fruit Served in a Watermelon Float with Dip Served in
Cantaloupe or Honeydew Half*
Fish-Shaped Cheese Crackers
Blue Gelatin Fish Bowl Served with Fish-Shaped Jelly Candy
Blue Hawaii Drinks or a large bucket filled with ice and soft drinks for
older children

Pineapple, Cheese and Cherry Skewers
Fresh or canned pineapple chunks, drained
1   large jar red maraschino cherries
1   pound chunk Cheddar cheese or pasteurized process cheese, cubed
1   fresh pineapple
1   box cocktail toothpicks or fondue skewers

Alternate pineapple, cheese and cherries on skewers. Place randomly in a
fresh pineapple.

Watermelon Float with Fresh Fruit
1   watermelon
1   bunch green seedless grapes
1   bunch red seedless grapes
Fresh strawberries
1   cantaloupe
1   honeydew melon

Wash all fruit well. Cut watermelon in half and cut as many balls as possible
from center of melon with a melon ball cutter. Hull out remainder of melon
to form basket. Zigzag cut around top with a large knife. Make melon balls
from honeydew and cantaloupe, saving half of either for dip serving bowl.
Zigzag cut the reserved half and hull out. Fill watermelon float with fruit.

Fruit Dip

1   tablespoon white corn syrup
1   large jar marshmallow cream
1   large container frozen whipped topping, thawed

Combine syrup and cream in a bowl. Fold in whipped topping, cover and refrigerate until ready to serve. Spoon into melon half and serve with fresh fruit.

Blue Gelatin Fish Bowl Sprinkled with Fish-Shaped Jelly Candy

1   clear glass fish bowl, washed
1   large box blue gelatin
1   bag fish-shaped jelly candy

Prepare gelatin according to package directions. Pour into bowl and chill until set. Sprinkle with candy before serving. Surround base of bowl with seashells.

DECORATIONS:

Use Luau theme paper plates, cups and napkins with wicker plate holders for an extra touch.

Cover tables with brightly colored tablecloths. Drape with fish nets and drape fish nets from patio or deck railings. Use fresh pineapples as centerpieces for tables. Scatter seashells and leis around the base of pineapples.

Place patio torches around for atmosphere.

Use lots of fresh flowers!

FUN AND GAMES:

As the children arrive, give the girls a grass skirt, leis and silk flowers for their hair; give the boys straw hats and leis.

Find a piñata at a party store and fill with favorite candy. Have Luau theme goody bags ready to fill.

Have a hula hoop contest to your favorite luau songs.

For younger children, have a fish pond filled with luau goodies or decorate plastic sunglasses with small shells, jewels and paint markers.

Star Studded Party

INVITATIONS:
Create your own invitations by making stars or movie tickets from construction paper.

MENU:
Video Cake
Popcorn
Hoagie Sandwiches
Trail Mix

Video Cake
1 box cake mix
1 can chocolate frosting
miniature marshmallows
1 tube of white prepared icing

> Happy
> Birthday
> #13
> starring
> Allison

Prepare cake mix and bake according to package directions, using a 13x9x2-inch baking dish. Place cake on platter or foil-covered cardboard. Spread chocolate frosting smoothly on top and sides of cake. Arrange marshmallows in row on each side of cake to resemble holes in strip of film. Using tube of frosting write a birthday "movie title" such as "Happy Birthday # (age)" and then "starring (child's name).'

DECORATIONS:
Decorate table with your favorite movie theater candies.

Use popcorn boxes with overflowing popcorn freshly popped. Set up director's chairs for additional seating.

FUN AND GAMES:
Sound tracks of favorite movies to set the mood.

Play charades acting out your favorite movies, movie stars and theme songs.

You could create your own movie, music video or commercial. Allow time at the end of party for viewing and signing autographs.

PARTY FAVORS:
Movie star sunglasses, discount movie coupons, and autograph books

Picnic Party

INVITATION:

Use a printed invitation with a red and white checked border or make your own on paper cut to look like watermelons, ladybugs or ants.

Sample Wording:
Recipe for Mary Ellen's 2nd Birthday Party:
Picnic cloths (red checks will do)
A bunch of ants - some Lady Bugs, too
Tons of family - lots of friends
One sunny day that never ends!
Join Mary Ellen in her back yard
Date _____
Time _____
For a picnic dinner and surprises!

MENU:

Cake and ice cream
Hot dogs, baked beans and chips
Caterpillar made of cupcakes - Decorate 1 cupcake with licorice sticks to make antenna and chocolate chips for the nose and mouth. Arrange other cupcakes behind it in the shape of a caterpillar. Give the decorated cupcake to the honoree.

DECORATIONS:

Use red and white checked tablecloths for children to sit on. Tie balloons to watermelon or ladybug piñatas and use as a centerpiece on each tablecloth. Picnic baskets and plastic insects also make great table accents.

FUN AND GAMES:

Outdoor Toys
Sidewalk Chalk

PARTY FAVORS:

Personalized picture frames - Use clear plastic frames and write the names with paint pens. Take pictures of the children during the party and send picture to them along with the thank-you note.

Miniature picnic baskets or clear treat bags. Write names on the outside with a paint pen. Cut a paper red and white checked table cloth into squares to line baskets or bags. Stuff bags with candy, stickers, bubbles, insect toys and gummy worms.

Beach Party

INVITATION:

Choose an invitation with a beach theme from the many now available at invitation stores or make your own by tracing a fish, sand bucket, palm tree, beach umbrella or beach ball. Hand write with a colored marker or a paint pen. Be sure to include on the invitation for children to bring their beach towels!

Sample Wording:
I love the sun, I love the sand,
I love my hat with the bright yellow band.
I love the surf, I love the sea,
So, Mommy and Daddy brought the beach to me!
Place come to my backyard beach
for my very first birthday party!
Date_____
Time_____
Don't forget your bathing suit and towel!

Love,
Mary Ellen

MENU:

Cake and Ice Cream
Peanut Butter and Jelly Sandwiches cut
into shapes with cookie cutters
Sand Cups*
Fruit Tray

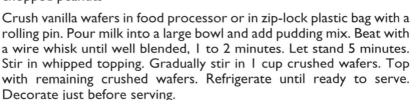

Sand Cups
35 vanilla wafers
2 cups cold milk
1 small package vanilla instant pudding
1½ cups frozen whipped topping, thawed

Decorations: miniature umbrellas, gummy sea shells, worms and sharks, candy stars, chopped peanuts

Crush vanilla wafers in food processor or in zip-lock plastic bag with a rolling pin. Pour milk into a large bowl and add pudding mix. Beat with a wire whisk until well blended, 1 to 2 minutes. Let stand 5 minutes. Stir in whipped topping. Gradually stir in 1 cup crushed wafers. Top with remaining crushed wafers. Refrigerate until ready to serve. Decorate just before serving.

Yield: 8 servings.

DECORATIONS:

Have a palm tree made out of green and yellow balloons - professional balloon companies can assemble these. Use small plastic wading pools for swimming. Put sand around pools and the palm tree.

Piñatas are great for centerpieces decorated with balloons.

Cut a wave shape into the top of blue construction paper to use as a place mat. Write names on the mats and have them laminated.

FUN AND GAMES:

Let the children play in the sand and the pools until it's time to eat and open presents.

PARTY FAVORS:

Plastic sand buckets with guests' names written on them with a paint pen. Fill with candy, stickers, sunglasses, bubbles and beach or pool toys.

Easter Party

INVITATIONS:

To make your own, fold pastel construction paper in half and cut into egg shapes. Decorate with stripes, stars and dots. Store-bought invitations with Easter themes are also available.

MENU:

Bunny Cake or Decorated Easter Cake

Carrot Sticks and Dip

Jelly Bean Baskets

Pink Lemonade

Bunny Cake

1 box cake mix
2 cans white frosting
red food coloring
flaked coconut
licorice laces
jelly beans

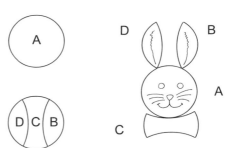

Prepare cake mix according to package directions, baking in 2 round 9-inch baking pans. Allow to cool. Place cake on foil-covered cardboard. Cut 1 layer according to illustration. Assemble cake pieces to form bunny head. Tint small amount of frosting to pink shade. Spread pink frosting in center of ears; frost bow tie with either white or pink frosting. Sprinkle coconut on face and ears. Arrange licorice and other candies on frosting for facial features. You can use chocolate frosting for a chocolate bunny! Have fun decorating!

DECORATIONS:

Make an Easter Tree by painting a tree branch white and securing it in a decorated flowerpot with florists clay. Punch holes in each end of an egg with an ice pick, blow out inside, rinse well and boil. Dye pastel colors and glue pastel ribbons to one end of egg. Tie onto tree. Plastic eggs may also be used.

Placemats—Large construction paper eggs, gaily decorated with each child's name.

FUN AND GAMES:

Have an Easter Egg hunt. Give prizes to who finds the most eggs and the least eggs.

Jelly bean exchange. Give each child a dozen jelly beans. The object of the game is to get as many of one color as he or she can by trading. Set a timer for 3 minutes and let the game begin.

PARTY FAVORS:

Fill miniature baskets with multicolored jelly beans wrapped in plastic wrap.

Come to the Big Top

INVITATIONS:

Design a ticket reading "Admit One to the Big Top." Include party particulars: address, date, time and host. Enclose a balloon, piece of gum or confetti in the invitation. You might want to ask the children to dress in a costume of something or someone they might see at a circus.

MENU:

Popcorn
Big Top Birthday or Ice Cream Cone Cupcakes*
Clown Ice Cream Faces*
Hot Dogs and Trimmings

Ice Cream Cone Cupcakes
1 box chocolate, yellow or white cake mix
Flat bottom ice cream cones
Frosting

Prepare cake mix according to package directions. Spoon batter into cones, filling three-quarters full. Place in muffin pans and bake according to package directions. Cool, frost and decorate.

Yield: 1½ to 2 dozen.

Clown Ice Cream Balls
Ice cream
Paper doilies
Ice cream cones
Chocolate drops
Red hot candies
Can of colored frosting or whipped cream (pressurized)

Scoop out ice cream balls and place on doilies. Place cone on each ball for clown's pointed hat. Make eyes with chocolate drops and a mouth with the red hot candies. Use frosting or whipped cream to make a scalloped clown's collar around base of ball. May be made ahead and frozen.

DECORATIONS:

Balloons! Balloons! Balloons!

Use stuffed animals sitting around room for decorations.

Use boxes of animal crackers for table decorations or party favors.

String twisted crepe paper from light fixture to ends of table to look like a big top tent.

FUN AND GAMES:

Play circus music as your guests arrive. Use it for musical chairs also.

Have a teenaged helper dress as a clown or hire a real clown.

Rent a cotton candy machine, moonwalk, etc. to create a circus atmosphere.

Pass out musical instruments and let the clown lead a circus band.

PARTY FAVORS:

Animal crackers in circus car boxes.

Balloons

Fill paper bags with popcorn or peanuts and tie with raffia.

Red, White and Blue Picnic – Fourth of July Celebration or Birthday

INVITATIONS:

Can be store bought with Fourth of July theme or make invitations out of blue construction paper. Draw or glue American flag in the center of paper. Sprinkle a few gold stars here and about. Fold paper in thirds; write party information inside in white ink on the side flaps. Seal with red sealing wax.

MENU:

Barbecue Chicken or Ribs
Potato Salad
Roasted Corn
Watermelon
Homemade Ice Cream
Lemonade

DECORATIONS:

Greet guests with the American flag at entrance of party area. Use a red, white and blue theme, with red and white checked tablecloths and red bandanas tied around silverware as napkins. Use seasonal flowers with small American flags inserted for centerpieces. Decorate a large cardboard box decorated with the words "Keep America Beautiful" to use for cleanup.

FUN AND GAMES:

Have relay races, sack races, egg rolls, etc.
Have a bike parade for the children.
Provide crepe paper streamers, balloons and tin cans to decorate the bicycles and have a contest for the best-decorated bike. Have the winner lead the parade.

PARTY FAVORS:

Small American flags, patriotic hats

Members
And Index

 # Menu/Party Ideas

Current and Former Members

Mrs. Charles Aaron
Adelle Aldridge
Tammy Allen
Sue Anderson
Tammy Anderson
Mary Andreae
Priscilla Bagwell
Velinda Bagwell
Mrs. George Baker
Nancy Barker
Laverne Barnard
Betsy Bennett
Cathy Beuoy
Wanda Black
Lillian Black
Ann Boatwright
Brenda Bobo
Tricia Bobo
Regina Bowling
Willie Ruth Brannon
Valeria Breen
Janet Bright
Martha Bryan
Sue Bryan
Lynn Burden
Leona Burden
Mrs. Richard Byrd
Gwen Campbell
Joanne Campbell
Vicki Campbell
Luann Campbell
Lem Carter
Mrs. Paul Christian
Barbara Clayton
Annette Clayton
Jo Ann Cleveland
Mary Jane Clinton
Mrs. Gene Cobb
Patsy Coble

Sandra Coleman
Pam Cooper
Mrs. Y. Z. Collins
Sue Cooley
Donna Copeland
Barbara Cordes
Sally Cox
Jan Cox
Martha Crawford
Barbara Creech
Laura Creel
Carol Davis
Judy Davis
Mary Alice Dennis
Mrs. Jack Dillard
Mrs. T. M. Dorman
Macie Drake
Beth Dumas
Mrs. Joseph Dyar
Roberta Eastep
Ludie Elrod
Patricia Elrod
Hilda Estes
Mrs. John Faught
Clarice Fowler
Dianne Fowler
Cathy Freeman
Judy Gibbs
Judy Glenn
Cynthia Green
Joyce Grobmeyer
Peggy Gunter
Betty Hamilton
Martha Hamilton
Myra Hammond
Martha Handschumacher
Candace Hargraves
Robbie Harris
Linda Hart

Lisa Hart
Kelly Hawk
Joanie Helms
Julene Helms
Diana Henson
Carrie Hill
Sara Hill
Flora Ann Hinds
Harriet Holder
Mary Hollis
Kim Holmes
Mrs. Byron Holloway
Pam Hornsby
Doris Hudson
Linda Hudson
Sarah Hudson
Helen Hughes
Luanne Humphries
Gail Hunt
Toni Hunt
Patty Hymer
Suzanne Ingram
Gwen Jockell
Sherry Johnson
Lynette Johnston
Jacqueline Jones
Sherry Kelly
Ruth Kelly
Mrs. Gerald Kemper
Ruth Kennamer
Ann Key
Sherri King
Toby King
Wendy King
Jan Kitchens
Mildred LaGrone
Mrs. Luther Latham
Avice Ledbetter
Mary Limperis
Ava Ruth Linn
Susan Linn
Gail Lueker
Lois Lyons

Kay Mardis
Mrs. David Marion
Vernon Marshall
Barbara Martin
Mrs. Buddy Martin
Mrs. John Martin
Mrs. W. C. Martin
Pat Martin
Alicia Maze
Lisa Maze
Pat McCoy
Mrs. Charles McDonald
Elaine McDonald
Ginney McDonald
Jane McDonald
Charlene McGee
Mrs. R. C. McGhee
Bonnie McInnis
Judy McKenzie
Mildred Meharg
Jerrie Meinert
Ann Melton
Mrs. Dowling Miller
Pam Mills
Jane Mizell
Joyce Moore
Dawn Morgan
Mary Lillian Morris
Amy Moss
Janice Moss
Paula Moss
Brenda Mullis
Sally Mullis
Irma Murphree
Carolyn Nelson
Sandra NeSmith
Cheryl Nichols
Sylvia Nilson
Jean Nixon
Mrs. Dick Norton
Annette O'Dell
Joyce Oliver
Mrs. T. M. Parker

Gerri Passinissi
Carolyn Patterson
Lindy Patterson
Toots Peterson
Nona Porch
Myra Porter
Joy Privett
Maxine Putnam
Mrs. Lester Ralph
Catherine Reed
Mrs. Ewell Reed
Mrs. Jimmy Rees
Martha Jean Reynolds
Doris Rice
Carol Richards
Mrs. William A. Riley
Duell Saylor
Pamela Schmidt
Myrna Shores
Mrs. Kyle Sirmon
Jackie Smalley
Louise Smalley
Mary Nell Smalley
Brenda Smith
Mrs. Frank Smith
Jane Smith
Ursula Smith
Gail Sparks
Mrs. John Steed
Cathy Stewart
Val Stewart
Mrs. James Stisher
Joanne Stisher
Saundra Stisher
Cathy Strawn
Diane Strickland
Kaye Stricklend
Joy Talley

Imogene Tate
Becky Taylor
Dian Taylor
Peggy Taylor
Donna Taylor
Kristy Thomas
Linda Thompson
Theresa Thornhill
Jewell Thrasher
Joette Thrower
Wanda Thrower
Dean Thurman
Andreé Tidmore
Rava Tinley
Barbara Trimble
Hannah Tyler
Snookie Vaughn
Lisa Vickers
Marsha Vickers
Tawayna Vickers
Carolyn Walden
Sandra Walker
Mrs. Verbon Walker
Sheila Watkins
Betty Weaver
Mrs. Richard Webster
Penny Welicki
Ramona Whisenant
Gail White
Jackie Wilks
Laura Williams
Norma Williams
Susan Willis
Thora Wisener
Mrs. James Woolbright
Carol Wynn
Beverly Zehr

 After a diligent search of past records, we regret if the name of any former member has been omitted.

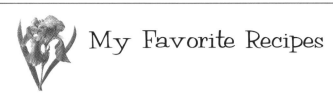# My Favorite Recipes

A

B

C

CAKES, see Desserts

CANTALOUPE

CASSEROLES

R

S

Simple Pleasures
Arab Mothers' Club
P.O. Box 884 • Arab, Alabama 35016

Please send _____ copy(ies) (includes sales tax) @ $16.95 each _____

Shipping and handling @ $ 3.50 each _____

Name _____

Address _____

City _____ State _____ Zip _____

Make checks payable to Arab Mothers' Club Cookbook

Simple Pleasures
Arab Mothers' Club
P.O. Box 884 • Arab, Alabama 35016

Please send _____ copy(ies) (includes sales tax) @ $16.95 each _____

Shipping and handling @ $ 3.50 each _____

Name _____

Address _____

City _____ State _____ Zip _____

Make checks payable to Arab Mothers' Club Cookbook

Simple Pleasures
Arab Mothers' Club
P.O. Box 884 • Arab, Alabama 35016

Please send _____ copy(ies) (includes sales tax) @ $16.95 each _____

Shipping and handling @ $ 3.50 each _____

Name _____

Address _____

City _____ State _____ Zip _____

Make checks payable to Arab Mothers' Club Cookbook

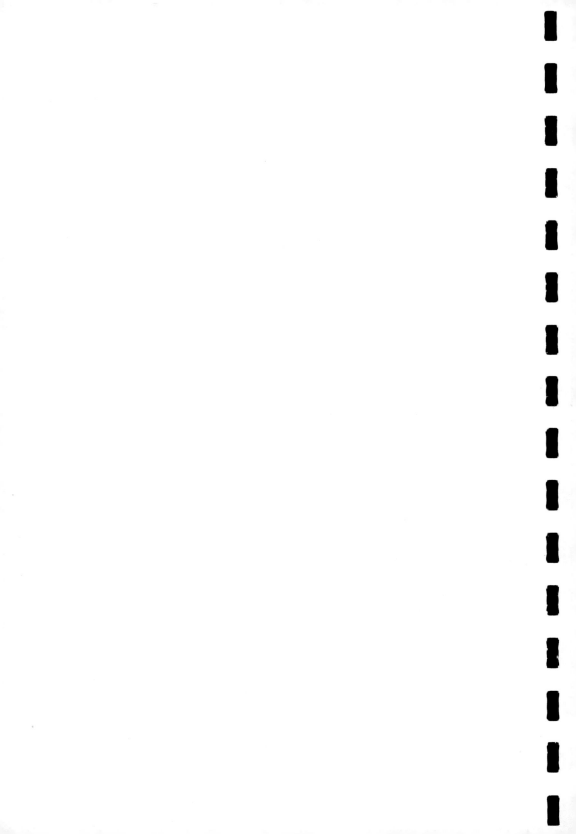